TOSHIBA

The Concise Guide to
Microsoft®
Windows™ 3.1

PUBLISHED BY
Microsoft Press
A Division of Microsoft Corporation
One Microsoft Way
Redmond, Washington 98052-6399

Library of Congress Cataloging-in-Publication Data

Jamsa, Kris A.
   Concise guide to Microsoft Windows 3.1 / Kris Jamsa.
      p. cm.
   Includes index.
   ISBN 1-55615-470-4
   1. Microsoft Windows (Computer program)   I. Title.
QA76.76.W56J365 1992
005.4'3--dc20   92-761
                               CIP

Printed and bound in the United States of America.

1 2 3 4 5 6 7 8 9 RDRD 7 6 5 4 3 2

Distributed to the book trade in Canada by Macmillan of Canada,
a division of Canada Publishing Corporation.

Distributed to the book trade outside the United States and Canada by Penguin Books Ltd.

Penguin Books Ltd., Harmondsworth, Middlesex, England
Penguin Books Australia Ltd., Ringwood, Victoria, Australia
Penguin Books N.Z. Ltd., 182-190 Wairau Road, Auckland 10, New Zealand

British Cataloging-in-Publication Data available.

TrueType® is a registered trademark of Apple Computer, Inc. i486® and Intel® are registered trademarks of Intel Corporation. IBM® is a registered trademark of International Business Machines Corporation. Microsoft®, Microsoft Press®, and MS-DOS® are registered trademarks and Windows™ is a trademark of Microsoft Corporation. Paintbrush™ is a trademark of Z Soft Corporation.

Acquisitions Editor: Michael Halvorson
Project Editor: Casey D. Doyle
Technical Editor: Jim Fuchs

Contents

Introduction

In 1981, IBM released its first personal computer, Microsoft released MS-DOS, and the PC revolution began. Throughout the 1980s, millions of users learned to issue a variety of MS-DOS commands and to use a variety of applications.

By the end of the decade, most users had a word processor, a spreadsheet, and possibly a database application they used regularly. In fact, most users were seeking an easy way to exchange information between applications—a method that would eliminate the need to end one application before looking up information stored by another.

In 1990, Microsoft introduced Windows 3.0, a program designed to maximize productivity. Windows 3.0 made computers easier to use, applications easier to learn, and allowed several applications to run at the same time. And—perhaps more importantly—it provided a simple means of information exchange between applications. Windows is a *graphical environment*: Its menus, icons (meaningful symbols), and dialog boxes replace the often cryptic commands that MS-DOS requires.

In 1992, Microsoft released Windows 3.1, which provides object links to help applications share data; TrueType fonts, which you can size to any height and print exactly as they appear on the screen; enhanced help; and even an online tutorial. Windows 3.1 brings multimedia to the PC world. If your PC has a sound board, a CD-ROM, and a MIDI device, Windows 3.1 provides you with the ability to record, edit, and play video and sounds. In addition, Windows 3.1 lets you assign specific sounds to various system events.

Just as the 1980s saw the PC revolution, the 1990s are seeing the Windows revolution.

How to Use This Book

This book is bursting at the bindings with information you need to put Windows to use:

■ Part I defines the elements of a window and describes how to use them with both a mouse and a keyboard. It also introduces the extensive online help feature Windows provides.

- Part II describes how to use the Windows Program Manager to run applications. The Program Manager organizes applications into groups, simplifying the selection of related applications, such as a word processor and a spreadsheet. It also introduces the File Manager, which displays directory listings and performs essential file operations such as Copy, Rename, and Delete, and describes how to use the PIF Editor and Clipboard Viewer. Part II also describes the Print Manager, which controls printer output, and the Task List, which moves you quickly among running applications.

- Part III explains how to customize Windows according to hardware needs (printer types, port usage, and network) and personal preference (window colors, keyboard speed, cursor blink rate, and so on).

- Part IV introduces the *desktop accessories* available with Windows, powerful programs that perform like many of the items commonly found on your desk such as a clock, notepad, calculator, calendar, and appointment book.

- Part V introduces the Windows games Solitaire and Minesweeper.

Four appendixes provide you with special information:

- Appendix A walks you through installing Windows.

- Appendix B provides an easy-to-read list of keyboard shortcuts used within Windows.

- Appendix C explores memory and system settings.

- Appendix D is a glossary that contains terms commonly used in Windows.

In short, this reference contains all the steps you need to take, not just to get Windows started, but to really put Windows to work.

PART I

Essential Operations in Windows

This book assumes that Microsoft Windows is installed on your computer and that you're ready to start it and become acquainted with the basics of Windows. If Windows is not yet installed on your computer, you can get all the installation information you need by turning to Appendix A, "Installing Windows."

STARTING WINDOWS

To start Windows, type the following command at the MS-DOS prompt (C:\>), pressing Enter as shown:

```
WIN <Enter>
```

The Windows *desktop*, similar to Figure 1-1, appears on your screen. (If you get the message *Bad command or filename*, see Appendix A, "Installing Windows," for instructions on adding the Windows subdirectory to your computer's search path.)

RUNNING THE WINDOWS ONLINE TUTORIAL

Windows 3.1 provides an online tutorial that teaches you how to use a mouse with Windows. To run the tutorial, do this:

 Choose Windows Tutorial from Program Manager's Help menu.

The Tutorial displays a series of windows, each containing easy-to-follow instructions. Follow the instructions to complete the tutorial, or press the Esc key to quit (you might need to complete the on-screen instructions before you can quit the tutorial).

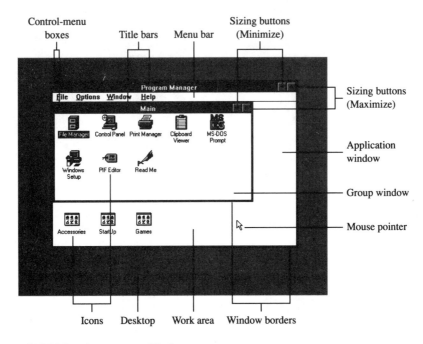

FIGURE 1-1. *After you start Windows, your screen looks something like this.*

WINDOWS AT A GLANCE

A *window* is simply a framed region on the screen. Each window contains the following elements (as shown in Figure 1-1):

- *Window borders* are the four edges that define the border of a window.
- The *title bar* is the area directly below the window's top border. The title bar displays the window's name.
- The *control-menu box* is in the upper left corner of the window and has an inner rectangle.
- The *mouse pointer* indicates where the mouse is currently positioned on the screen.
- *Sizing buttons (Minimize/Maximize)* are buttons in the upper right corner of the window that minimize or maximize the window.
- The *mouse pointer* indicates where the mouse is currently positioned on the screen.
- The *menu bar* is the area under the title bar. The menu bar provides access to most of an application's commands.

- The *work area* is the area inside a window.

- *Icons* are visual representations of minimized windows, applications, or documents.

Windows supports three kinds of windows: *application windows*, and subwindows within application windows called *document windows*. Windows also supports a special type of document window called a *group window*, which contains application icons. In Figure 1-1, Program

Getting Around the Screen: A Primer

This book describes a variety of basic operations you can do in Windows. All can be carried out with a mouse or from the keyboard. (A mouse is strongly recommended, however.) The following symbols will help you find the instructions you need at a glance:

   Instructions for mouse users

   Instructions for keyboard users

In addition, mouse users should know how to perform the following actions. (Typical uses for these actions are noted in parentheses.)

To click	Position the tip of the mouse pointer over the specified element, and then press and release the left mouse button one time. (Selecting windows, icons, or files in a list; selecting dialog box options.)
To double-click	Position the tip of the mouse pointer over the specified element, and then press and release the left mouse button twice in quick succession. (Expanding icons; executing applications; choosing items from a list.)
To drag	Position the tip of the mouse pointer over the specified element, hold down the left mouse button, and move the mouse. The mouse pointer moves, dragging the element. Move the element to the desired location and release the left mouse button. (Moving windows or icons; resizing windows.)

Keyboard users should know how to use *keyboard shortcuts*. A keyboard shortcut is a single keystroke or a combination of keystrokes that execute a command directly. For example, the keyboard shortcut *Ctrl+F4* provides the same result as choosing Close from the Control menu of the Main window. Appendix B lists the keyboard shortcuts for a variety of tasks.

Manager is an application window, and Main is a group window. Also note the File Manager application icon, which is highlighted.

WORKING WITH ICONS

As shown in Figure 1-1, when you start Windows, a number of icons (graphical symbols of an application or a minimized window) appear. To work with an icon, you expand it; that is, you cause the icon to become a window residing on the desktop.

To expand an icon, follow these steps:

 Double-click on the icon.

 For an application icon sitting on the desktop, repeatedly press Alt+Esc until the icon's name is selected, and then press Enter, or press Alt+Spacebar, R.

For an icon sitting within a group window, use the arrow keys to select the icon, and then press Enter.

For a document or group icon, repeatedly press Ctrl+F6 until the icon is selected, and then press Enter.

SELECTING A WINDOW

When your screen contains several application windows, you can select the one you want by clicking on the window or by repeatedly pressing Alt+Esc. You can tell when a window is selected because its borders and menu bar darken.

WORKING WITH MENUS

Immediately below an application window's title bar is a menu bar. The menu bar lists the names of one or more *menus* (lists of related commands). For example, the Program Manager menu bar contains the File, Options, Window, and Help menus.

Opening a Menu

To open a menu, follow these steps:

Click on the menu name.

Press Alt+*X*, where *X* is the key that represents the desired menu name. (Each menu name has an underlined character that represents the menu. For example, press Alt+F to open the File menu.)

When you open a menu, a list of *commands* appears, as shown in Figure 1-2.

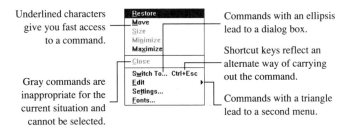

Underlined characters give you fast access to a command.

Gray commands are inappropriate for the current situation and cannot be selected.

Commands with an ellipsis lead to a dialog box.

Shortcut keys reflect an alternate way of carrying out the command.

Commands with a triangle lead to a second menu.

FIGURE 1-2. *A sample open menu.*

Selecting a Command

To select a command from a command menu, follow these steps:

Click on the command.

Press *X*, where *X* is the letter underlined in the command. If the command has no underlined letter, use the arrow keys to highlight the command, and then press Enter.

Closing a Menu

To close a menu without selecting a command, click on a location outside of the menu, or press the Esc key.

WORKING WITH DIALOG BOXES

A *dialog box* is a window that frequently provides information and always requests a user response. Figure 1-3 shows a sample dialog box that helps you set up your desktop. A dialog box might simply display a status message, waiting until you select OK, or it might ask you to specify a filename or other information.

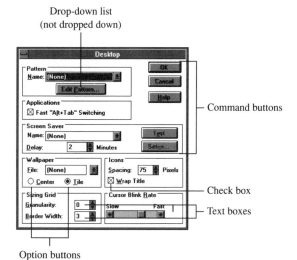

FIGURE 1-3. *A sample dialog box.*

Dialog boxes can contain several fields of information, as described in the following paragraphs. To select a field within a dialog box, follow these steps:

 Click on the desired field.

 Press Alt+*X*, where *X* is the letter underlined in the field name. Use the Tab key to advance from one dialog box field to the next. Use Shift+Tab to return to the previous field.

Command buttons A command button directs a dialog box to perform a specific action.

Text box A text box lets you type in a text string, such as a filename. Sometimes a text box contains default text (which might be highlighted). To enter different text, simply type in the new text, which replaces the old text automatically. To make minor changes to the default text, press the left arrow key, and edit the text using the Backspace, Delete, and arrow keys.

List box A list box provides you with a list of options. If the list contains more options than the box can display, the box contains a scroll bar. To choose an option, follow these steps:

Double-click on the option.

 Use the arrow keys to select the option, and then press Enter.

If the list lets you select multiple options, check the documentation that came with the application for instructions on selecting more than one.

Drop-down list Dialog boxes use drop-down lists when there's not enough room for a list box. Figure 1-4 shows a sample dialog box with a drop-down list. To drop down the list, follow these steps:

 Click on the downward pointing arrow at the right of the list.

 Select the drop-down list, and then press Alt+Down arrow.

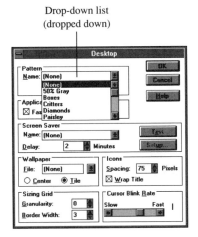

FIGURE 1-4. *A dialog box with a dropped-down list.*

Option button When the options you can select from are mutually exclusive—that is, when you are allowed to select only one of them at a time—they are grouped together as *option buttons*. Option buttons appear as circles with text next to them. One option in each group (the currently selected option) has a darkened circle. Gray or dimmed options are inappropriate for the current situation and cannot be selected.

To select an option button, follow these steps:

 Click on the option button.

 Press Alt+*X*, where *X* is the letter underlined in the option name. If the option name doesn't have an underlined letter, press the Tab key until one of the option names is encircled by a dotted line. Use the arrow keys to move the darkened circle to the desired option.

Check box Options that can be individually turned on or off are displayed as check boxes. When a check box is empty, the option is off. An X in the check box indicates that the option is selected. Gray or dimmed options are inappropriate for the current situation and cannot be selected.

To select or deselect a check box, follow these steps:

 Click on the check box.

 Press Alt+*X*, where *X* is the letter underlined in the check box name. If the check box name doesn't have an underlined letter, press the Tab key until the option is encircled by a dotted line, and then press the Spacebar.

SCROLLING FOR INFORMATION

When an application contains more information than can fit in a window, vertical and horizontal scroll bars appear along the window's right and bottom edges, as shown in Figure 1-5. Within the scroll bars, a *scroll box* moves to reflect your relative position within the document. To use scroll bars, follow these steps:

- To move a short distance, click on the up and down or left and right arrows at each end of the scroll bar.
- To move up by approximately one screen, click on the vertical scroll bar above the scroll box. To move down by approximately one screen, click on the vertical scroll bar below the scroll box. To move to the left by approximately one screen, click on the horizontal scroll bar to the left of

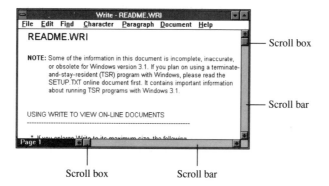

FIGURE 1-5. *Scroll bars and scroll boxes help you work within your document.*

the scroll box. To move to the right by approximately one screen, click on the horizontal scroll bar to the right of the scroll box.

■ To move to a specific location, drag the scroll box along the scroll bar to quickly scan through the window's contents.

 Use the arrow keys or the PgUp and PgDn keys to scroll through the window's contents.

SIZING A WINDOW

Windows provides you with several ways to increase and decrease the size of a window.

Minimizing a Window

To minimize a window—that is, to reduce it to an icon—follow these steps:

 Click on the Minimize button (a downward-pointing triangle) in the upper right corner of the window.

 For an application window, press Alt+Spacebar, N.

For a document or group window, press Alt+Hyphen, N.

Restoring a Minimized Window

To restore a minimized window—that is, to expand an icon to a window—perform the steps that follow.

Double-click on the icon.

For an icon on the desktop, press Alt+Spacebar, R.

For a document or group icon, press Alt+Hyphen, R.

Maximizing a Window

To maximize a window—that is, to enlarge it to the fullest possible size—follow these steps:

Click on the Maximize button (an upward-pointing triangle) in the upper right corner of the window.

For an application window, press Alt+Spacebar, X.

For a document or group window, press Alt+Hyphen, X.

Restoring a Maximized Window

When you maximize a window, that window's Maximize button becomes a Restore button. To restore a window to its previous size, follow these steps:

Click on the Restore button (an upward-pointing triangle sitting on top of a downward-pointing triangle).

For an application window, press Alt+Spacebar, R.

For a document or group window, press Alt+Hyphen, R.

Incrementally Sizing a Window

To stretch or compress a window, follow these steps:

Drag a window border to the desired size. When you release the mouse button, Windows expands or shrinks the window to fill the new area.

- To change window height, drag the window's top or bottom border.

- To change window width, drag the window's left or right border.

- To change both height and width, drag a corner of two borders.

1. For an application window, press Alt+Spacebar, S.

   For a document or group window, press Alt+Hyphen, S.

2. Press the arrow key that corresponds to the window border you want to change. The up arrow key corresponds to the top border, the down arrow key corresponds to the bottom border, the right arrow key corresponds to the right border, and the left arrow key corresponds to the left border. (To change both height and width at the same time, press two arrow keys simultaneously.)

3. Using the arrow keys, move the border to the desired location and press Enter. When you press Enter, Windows expands or shrinks the window to fill the new area.

MOVING A WINDOW

One of the benefits of the Windows desktop is that it allows you to move your work around to suit your needs and priorities. To move a window, follow these steps:

Drag the title bar of the window to the desired location.

1. For an application window, press Alt+Spacebar, M.

   For a document or group window, press Alt+Hyphen, M.

2. Use the arrow keys to move the window to the location you desire, and then press Enter.

NOTE: *When you move a window, Windows moves only an outline of the window until you release the mouse button or press Enter.*

CLOSING A WINDOW

When you close an application window, the corresponding application stops. If you have made changes and have not yet saved the changes on disk, a dialog box appears asking whether you want to save the changes.

To close a window, follow these steps:

Double-click on the window's Control menu box.

For an application window, press Alt+Spacebar, C. For a document or group window, press Alt+Hyphen, C.

USING THE CONTROL MENU

Every window has a *Control menu*, which contains commands that let you move, size, or close a window by using the keyboard (Figure 1-6).

FIGURE 1-6. *A typical Control menu.*

To open the Control menu, follow these steps:

   Click on the Control menu box in the window's upper left corner adjacent to the menu bar.

   For an application window, press Alt+Spacebar. For a document or group window, press Alt+Hyphen.

The following list briefly describes each Control menu command:

Command	Function
Restore	Restores a window to its previous size following a minimize or maximize operation
Move	Lets you move the window using the arrow keys
Size	Lets you change the window's size using the arrow keys
Minimize	Reduces the window to an icon
Maximize	Expands the window to full size
Close	Closes the window
Switch To	Opens the Task List dialog box, which lets you select another running application
Next	Selects the next open document or group window within an application window

IF YOU NEED HELP

To help you quickly resolve problems and to answer your questions, Windows provides online help that you can use from within Windows. Simply use one of the following techniques:

- Choose a command from the Help menu on the menu bar.
- Press F1 while working within an application window.
- Choose the Help button in a dialog box.

The following list describes the Help commands provided by most applications:

Command	Function
Contents	Opens a window showing the table of contents for topics concerning the selected application
Search for Help On	Opens a dialog box that allows you to type a subject name for which Windows displays a list of related help topics
How to Use Help	Opens a window showing explanatory text about Window's online help
About	Opens a window showing copyright information for the selected application

When you select a command from the Help menu or when you press F1, a window appears with help text and the following buttons (Figure 1-7). (Dimmed buttons are inappropriate for the current situation and cannot be selected.)

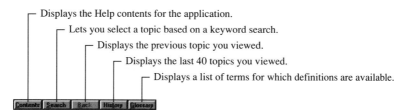

FIGURE 1-7. *The help buttons.*

To choose a help button, follow these steps:

    Click on the help button.

    Press Alt+*X*, where *X* is the letter underlined in the button name.

Accessing Expanded Help

Additional information is available for terms that are underlined in the help text. To obtain additional information, perform the steps that follow.

Click on the underlined term.

 Press the Tab key to highlight the term, and then press Enter.

Accessing Definitions

Definitions are available for terms that have a dotted underline in the help text. To see the definition of the term, follow these steps:

 Click on the term.

 Press the Tab key to highlight the term, and then press Enter.

If you encounter a term you don't understand, you can look it up using the Glossary button. To choose the Glossary button, follow these steps:

 Click on the Glossary button.

 Press Alt+G.

A glossary dialog box similar to the one shown in Figure 1-8 appears.

FIGURE 1-8. *Help's glossary window.*

To view the definition of a specific term, follow these steps:

  1. If necessary, drag the scroll box within the scroll bar to bring the term into view.

2. Click on the term.

1. If necessary, use the PgUp and PgDn keys to bring the term into view.

2. Press the Tab key to highlight the term, and then press Enter.

Help displays the term's definition in a pop up window similar to the one shown in Figure 1-9.

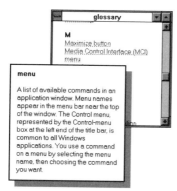

FIGURE 1-9. *A glossary definition in a pop up window.*

To remove the pop up window, click your mouse, or press any key. To close the glossary window, either double-click on the glossary window's Control menu box, or press Alt+F4.

Printing a Help Topic

To print the help topic, choose Print Topic from Help's File menu.

Choose Print Setup from Help's File menu if you want to select a printer other than the default printer, change the paper size or tray, change the print orientation (portrait or landscape), or change the print intensity for graphics. (You learn about these options in "Configuring a Printer" in Part III. Most users can simply use the default settings.)

Returning to Previous Help Topics

As you use Help to learn about various topics, there might be times when you want to return to a topic you were previously viewing. To do so, choose Back. Help displays the previous Help topic. If you choose Back again, Help returns to the topic you viewed before the current one. You can view as many as 40 previous topics in this manner.

Help's History button also lets you quickly return to a previous topic. When you choose History by clicking on the History button or by pressing

Alt+T, Help opens a History dialog box similar to Figure 1-10, which lists up to 40 previously viewed topics.

FIGURE 1-10. *The history dialog box.*

To return to a previous Help topic, follow these steps:

1. If necessary, drag the scroll box until the topic becomes visible.

2. Double-click on the topic.

Use the arrow keys to highlight the topic, and then press Enter.

To close the History dialog box without making a selection, double-click on its Control menu box or press Alt+F4.

Performing a Keyword Search

The Search button lets you search for help from a list of predefined key-words. To choose the Search button, click on the Search button, or press Alt+S.

When you choose the Search button, a dialog box appears, similar to Figure 1-11:

FIGURE 1-11. *The Search dialog box.*

The Search dialog box contains three fields: a text box near the top of the dialog box; a list box in the middle of the dialog box that contains all available keywords; and another list box at the bottom of the dialog box.

To search for a topic, follow these steps:

1. Select a keyword from the middle list box. (In addition to scrolling in the typical way, you can type the first letter or two of the desired keyword into the text box, and the middle text box moves to and highlights the first keyword that matches the letters you specified.)

2. If you find the keyword you desire, choose Go To. Help searches the help file for matching occurrences of the keyword and displays each match in the bottom list box.

3. If a reference in the bottom list box is of interest, double-click on the reference, or use the arrow keys to select it, and then press Enter.

Bookmarks

To help you learn efficiently as well as effectively, Windows provides a bookmark command that lets you mark your place in Help before you exit. Later—rather than browsing to find where you left off—you can return directly to the place you marked.

Defining a Bookmark

To define a bookmark, follow these steps:

1. Choose Define from Help's Bookmark menu, or press Alt+M, D. The Bookmark Define dialog box appears, which contains the current help topic as the bookmark name (Figure 1-12).

FIGURE 1-12. *The Bookmark Define dialog box.*

2. Choose OK to accept the current name, or edit the name to your liking, and then choose OK to store the bookmark.

Accessing a Bookmark

To return to a marked position, follow these steps:

1. Open the Bookmark menu. A numbered list appears of every bookmark you've defined. (The list appears underneath the Define command.)

2. Click on the desired bookmark, or press the number that corresponds to the desired bookmark. You can also highlight the bookmark with the arrow keys and press Enter.

Deleting a Bookmark

To delete a bookmark, follow these steps:

1. Open the Bookmark menu.

2. Choose Define.

3. Select the bookmark you want to delete.

4. Choose Delete.

5. Choose OK.

Annotations in Help Text

Help lets you *annotate* the help text. When you annotate help text, you place your own comments or reminders within the material.

Adding an annotation

To create a help annotation, follow these steps:

1. Choose Annotate from Help's Edit menu. Help opens the Annotate dialog box shown in Figure 1-13.

FIGURE 1-13. *Help's Annotate Dialog Box.*

2. Type in your own comments or reminders.

3. Choose Save.

After you annotate a topic, Help displays a paper clip in front of the topic's title as shown in Figure 1-14.

To display a topic's annotated text, click on the paper clip, or press the Tab key to highlight the paper clip, and then press Enter.

Help displays the annotated text in a dialog box similar to the one shown in Figure 1-13. To close the dialog box, choose Cancel or press Alt+F4.

Paper clip indicating an annotation.

FIGURE 1-14. *After you annotate a topic, it is displayed with a paper clip.*

Removing an annotation

To remove an annotation, follow these steps:

1. Click on the paper clip. Help displays the annotated text in a dialog box.
2. Choose Delete.

1. Press the Tab key to highlight the paper clip, and then press Enter. Help displays the annotated text in a dialog box.
2. Choose Delete by pressing Alt+D.

Exiting Online Help

To exit the online help, double-click on the Help window's Control menu button, or press Alt+F4.

EXITING WINDOWS

To exit Windows, follow these steps:

1. Close all open application windows, saving open files as necessary.
2. Choose Exit Windows from Program Manager's File menu. The Exit Windows dialog box appears (Figure 1-15), confirming that you want to exit.

FIGURE 1-15. *The Exit Windows dialog box.*

3. Choose OK.

PART II

Standard Applications
in Windows

There are several key applications in Windows you use often: the Program Manager, the File Manager, the Clipboard Viewer, the Print Manager, the Task List, and the PIF Editor. You learn about each of them in this section.

THE PROGRAM MANAGER

The most important application in Windows is the *Program Manager*. The Program Manager is the window from which you start your applications. (See Figure 2-1.)

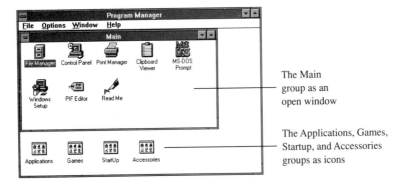

The Main group as an open window

The Applications, Games, Startup, and Accessories groups as icons

FIGURE 2-1. *A group can appear as a window or as an icon.*

Program Manager organizes applications into *groups*. A group can appear as an open window (called a *group window*) or as a minimized icon, as shown in Figure 2-1. A group window is a subwindow of the Program Manager window. Four groups—Main, Accessories, Games, and Startup—are standard groups in Windows:

Group	Contents
Main	Applications that let you configure your hardware and customize the Windows environment
Accessories	Applications that automate desktop tasks (Clock, Calculator, Notepad, and so on)
Games	The games Solitaire and Minesweeper
Startup	Programs you want to run each time Windows starts

You might also have one or more applications groups containing applications for Windows and MS-DOS.

Adding a Program Group

To help you organize your work effectively, the Program Manager lets you create your own groups. For example, you might create a group called Business, which might contain a spreadsheet, a word processor, and a project scheduler. To create a group, follow these steps:

1. Choose New from the Program Manager's File menu. The dialog box shown in Figure 2-2 appears.

FIGURE 2-2. *The New Program Object dialog box.*

2. Select Program Group, and choose OK. The dialog box shown in Figure 2-3 appears.

Temporarily Exiting Windows to MS-DOS

If you need to leave Windows temporarily and go to MS-DOS, you can do so easily by choosing the MS-DOS Prompt icon from the Main group. When you return to Windows, your previously open windows and files remain unchanged. To return to Windows from MS-DOS, use the Exit command as shown here:

```
C:\>EXIT
```

When you go to MS-DOS, do not turn off your computer without first returning to Windows and closing any applications that are running. This ensures that all files are saved correctly.

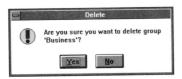

FIGURE 2-3. *The Program Group Properties dialog box.*

3. Type in the description you want to appear in this group window's title bar. Click on OK or press Enter.

Deleting a Program Group

If you decide a group is no longer necessary, you can delete it by following these steps:

1. Minimize and select the group you intend to delete. If you click on a group icon and its Control menu appears, click on the icon again to close the Control menu.

2. Choose Delete from the File menu, or press the Delete key. A dialog box similar to the one shown in Figure 2-4 appears.

FIGURE 2-4. *The Delete dialog box.*

3. If the dialog box displays the correct group name, choose Yes; otherwise, choose No.

Adding Applications to a Group

After you create a group, you can add applications to it. Likewise, if you buy a new application that runs under Windows (such as Microsoft Word for Windows), you can add it to an applications group. To add an application to a group, follow these steps:

1. Select the desired group window or icon.

2. Choose New from the File menu. The New Program Object dialog box appears (Figure 2-2).

3. Select Program Item, and choose OK. The dialog box shown in Figure 2-5 appears.

FIGURE 2-5. *The Program Item Properties dialog box.*

4. Type in the description you want to appear beneath the application's icon. Do *not* press Enter.

5. Move to the Command Line text box. Type in the application's complete filename, including the drive letter, pathname, and filename extension. Do *not* press Enter.

6. Move to the Working Directory text box and type in the directory where the application's data files are stored. Do *not* press Enter. You can leave this text box empty if the application has no data files or if the data files are stored in the same directory as the application.

7. Move to the Shortcut Key text box. A shortcut key is a key that, when pressed at the same time as Ctrl and Alt, makes the running application active. If you'd like to assign a shortcut key for this application, press the key you'd like to use as a shortcut key. Do *not* press Enter when you have finished.

8. If you'd like Windows to minimize the application when you run it, click on the Run Minimized check box, or press Alt+R.

9. Choose OK to add the application to the group.

Deleting Applications from a Group

To delete an application from a group, follow these steps:

1. Select the icon of the application you want to delete.

2. Choose Delete from the File menu, or press the Delete key. A dialog box similar to the one shown in Figure 2-6 appears.

FIGURE 2-6. *The Delete dialog box.*

3. If the item specified is the application you want to delete, choose Yes; otherwise, choose No.

Moving an Application from One Group to Another

To move an application from one group to another, follow these steps:

Drag the application's icon into the desired group window or atop the desired group icon.

1. Select the icon of the application you want to move.
2. Choose Move from the File menu. A dialog box similar to the one shown in Figure 2-7 appears.

FIGURE 2-7. *The Move Program Item dialog box.*

3. Press Alt+Down arrow key to open the drop-down list. Use the Up and Down arrow keys to select the group to which you want the application moved, and then press Enter.

Copying an Application from One Group to Another

To copy an application from one group to another, follow these steps:

Hold down the Ctrl key, and then drag the application's icon into the desired group window or atop the desired group icon.

1. Select the icon of the application you want to copy.
2. Choose Copy from the File menu. A dialog box similar to the one shown in Figure 2-8 appears.

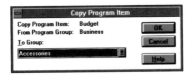

FIGURE 2-8. *The Copy Program Item dialog box.*

3. Press Alt+Down arrow key to open the drop-down list. Use the Up and Down arrow keys to select the group to which you want the application copied, and then press Enter.

Using the Startup Group

You might have one or more applications you want to run each time you start Windows. If you copy the application to the Startup group, as described above, Windows runs the application each time you start Windows.

Changing a Group Name

To change the name of a group, follow these steps:

1. Minimize and then select the desired group's window.
2. Choose Properties from the File menu. A dialog box similar to the one shown in Figure 2-9 appears.

FIGURE 2-9. *The Program Group Properties dialog box.*

3. Type a new group name in the Description text box, and choose OK.

Changing an Application's Description

To change an application's description, follow these steps:

1. Select the application's icon.
2. Choose Properties from the File menu. A dialog box similar to the one shown in Figure 2-10 appears.

FIGURE 2-10. *The Program Item Properties dialog box.*

3. Type in the new description. Choose OK.

Tiling or Cascading Group Windows

The Program Manager Window menu has two commands that help you view group windows. The first, Cascade, arranges group windows one on top of another, leaving the title bar of each window uncovered. The second, Tile, changes the size and position of each group window so that each is fully visible.

To arrange windows to best suit your needs, choose either Cascade or Tile from the Window menu.

Arranging Application and Group Icons

As you work with Windows, icons sometimes become disorganized within a group window. To tidy up the arrangement of icons, follow these steps:

1. Open the group window whose icons you want to arrange.

2. Choose Arrange Icons from the Window menu.

As you change the size of a group window, Windows might need to rearrange the icons so that you can view them. Choose Auto Arrange from the Options menu to have Windows automatically rearrange a resized group window's icons.

THE FILE MANAGER

The File Manager is a powerful application that lets you copy, delete, print, and rename files; run applications; and even perform disk operations such as formatting a new floppy disk.

The File Manager Screen

When you start the File Manager, a screen similar to the one in Figure 2-11 appears.

- *Disk-drive icons* represent the drives available to the File Manager. Drives are of the following types: floppy-disk drive, hard-disk drive, network drive, RAM-disk drive, and CD-ROM drive.

- The *disk volume label* is an optional 11-character name you can assign to a disk. (If your hard disk is unnamed, this field does not appear.)

- The *directory path and file specification* show the full pathname to the current directory as well as the specification for the files shown.

- The *directory tree* displays directories of the current drive. The File Manager lets you display either all, specific levels, or one level, of subdirectories in the directory tree.

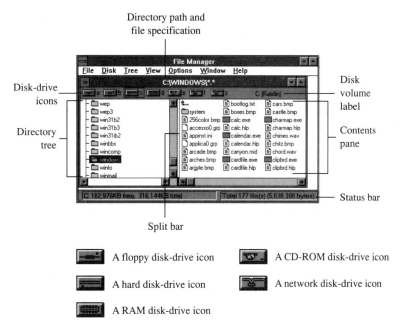

FIGURE 2-11. *Your screen looks like this after you start the File Manager.*

■ The *current directory* is the directory whose files the File Manager is currently displaying. The File Manager indicates the current directory by using an open file folder icon in the directory tree.

■ The *contents pane* shows the files and subdirectories in the current directory.

■ The *status bar* displays the amount of free space the current drive contains, as well as the number of files in, and the disk space consumed by, files in the current directory.

Changing Drives

You can change to any drive represented by a drive icon. To change to a drive, click on the drive's icon, or press Ctrl+*X*, where *X* is the letter of the drive you desire.

Changing Directories

To change to a different directory, click on the directory you desire or use the Up or Down arrow key to move the *selection frame* (the dotted rectangle) to the desired directory.

Expanding Directories

MS-DOS lets you store files in *directories*. Directories are organizational tools that allow you to group related files. Think of a directory as a folder inside a filing cabinet.

Directories can also contain other directories. A directory that contains another directory is called a *parent directory*. A directory within another directory is called a *subdirectory*.

The File Manager displays the contents of the current disk. Directories and subdirectories are displayed as icons that look like folders. (See Figure 2-11.) If a directory contains one or more subdirectories, its icon might contain a plus sign. If none of your directory icons contains a plus sign, choose Indicate Expandable Branches from the Tree menu.

Expanding a Single Directory

To expand a directory to reveal its subdirectories, perform these steps:

 Double-click on the directory's icon.

 Use the Up or Down arrow key to move the selection frame to the directory you desire, and then press Enter.

The File Manager expands the directory, showing its subdirectories and replacing the plus sign in the directory's icon with a minus sign.

To expand the directory to show all its subdirectories, including subdirectories within subdirectories, follow these steps:

1. Select the desired directory.
2. Choose Expand Branch from the Tree menu, or press the asterisk (∗) key.

Expanding the Entire Tree

To expand all directories on the current disk, choose Expand All from the Tree menu, or press Ctrl+∗.

Collapsing a Directory

By *collapsing* a directory, you hide its subdirectories. To collapse an expanded directory, follow these steps:

 Double-click on the directory's icon.

Select the directory with the Up or Down arrow key, and then press the minus sign key (–).

Viewing the Current Directory

The File Manager displays the current directory's files and subdirectories in the contents pane to the right of the directory tree. As you change directories, the File Manager updates the contents pane to display the files in the new current directory.

Each file in the contents pane has a corresponding icon that indicates the file type as shown here:

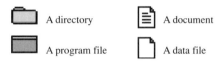

A directory   A document

A program file   A data file

Viewing Multiple Directories

Sometimes you might want to view the contents of two or more directories at the same time. To do so, open one or more additional directory windows. To open a directory window, choose New Window from the Window menu. The File Manager opens a second directory window as shown in Figure 2-12.

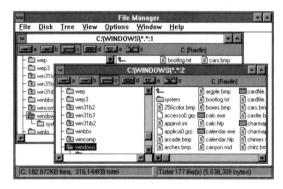

FIGURE 2-12. *The File Manager with two directory windows open.*

Within each directory window, you can change to any disk drive or directory. Additionally, the File Manager lets you move and copy files from one directory window to another.

TIP: *To open a new directory window for another drive, double-click on the drive's icon.*

Controlling the Display of Directory Windows

If you open multiple directory windows, you can move and size the windows as your needs require. The File Manager Window menu has two commands that help you view directory windows. The first, Cascade, arranges directory windows one on top of another, leaving the title bar of each window uncovered. The second, Tile, changes the size and position of each directory window so that each is fully visible.

To arrange windows to best suit your needs, choose either Cascade or Tile from the Window menu.

Closing a Directory Window

To close a directory window, follow these steps:

 Double-click on the window's Control menu box.

 Choose the Close option from the window's Control menu, or press Ctrl+F4.

Sometimes, rather than closing a directory window, you might want to temporarily minimize the window to an icon. When you do so, the directory window's icon appears at the bottom of the Program Manager window. To expand the icon, double-click on it or select the icon and press Alt+Hyphen, R.

Running Applications

When you open a directory window, the File Manager displays the files the directory contains. You can run applications and work with files listed in the directory window.

The File Manager provides several ways to run an application.

■ If the application's name appears in the contents pane, you can double-click on the application's icon, or follow these steps:

1. Press Tab to move the selection frame to the contents pane.

2. Use the arrow keys to move the selection frame to select the application.

3. Press Enter.

■ If the application's name does not appear in the directory window, follow these steps:

1. Choose Run from the File menu. A dialog box similar to the one in Figure 2-13 appears.

FIGURE 2-13. *The Run dialog box.*

2. Type in the path and name of the application you want to run, along with any additional information the application requires.

3. Select the Run Minimized box if you want the application to run in the background as an icon. Choose OK.

Changing Views

By default, a directory window contains a directory tree and a contents pane. The File Manager View menu has commands that let you display only the directory tree, only the contents pane, or both (the default) as described here.

Command	Function
Tree and Directory	Displays the directory tree and the contents pane
Tree Only	Displays only the directory tree
Directory Only	Displays only the contents pane

By default, the Program Manager divides a directory window into two panes. The left pane of the window is the directory tree, and the right pane is the contents pane. The File Manager lets you move the split bar that divides the window, increasing the size of one pane while decreasing the size of the other. To divide a directory window, follow these steps:

Drag the split bar to the left or to the right.

1. Choose the Split command from the View menu. A thick, black vertical bar appears in the middle of the directory window.

2. Use the Left or Right arrow key to move the bar to the left or to the right, and then press Enter.

Changing the File Information Displayed

By default, the File Manager displays only filenames and extensions in the contents pane. You can display other file characteristics by choosing commands from the View menu.

Seeing File Details

To display each file's name, extension, size, date and time stamp, and file attributes, choose All File Details from the View menu. To hide these details, choose Name from the View menu.

Customizing Directory Window Information

To have specific file information appear in the directory window, follow these steps:

1. Choose Partial Details from the View menu. A dialog box similar to the one in Figure 2-14 appears.

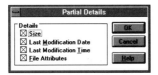

FIGURE 2-14. *The Partial Details dialog box.*

2. Select the file details you want the File Manager to display.

3. Choose OK.

Changing the Order of Directory Window Contents

Within a directory window, a list of directories followed by a list of filenames appears. Both the directory list and the filename list are sorted in alphabetic order. You can sort the files by Type (extension), Size, or Date by choosing the appropriate command from the View menu.

Restricting the File Types Displayed

By default, a directory window displays the name of every type of file in the directory. To restrict which file types appear, follow these steps:

1. Choose By File Type from the View menu. A dialog box similar to the one in Figure 2-15 appears.

2. Type in the wildcard pattern that corresponds to the files you want to display.

3. Select the check boxes of the file types you want to display, or deselect the file types you don't want to display.

FIGURE 2-15. *The By File Type dialog box.*

4. Press Enter or choose OK.

Selecting Multiple Files

When you need to select more than one file, you can use one of several methods, depending on how the files are arranged in the contents pane.

Selecting Consecutive Files

To select files whose names appear consecutively in the contents pane, follow these steps:

 Click on the first filename in the group. Hold down the Shift key, and click on the last filename in the group.

 Select the first file in the group. Hold down the Shift key, and use the arrow keys to select the remaining files in the group.

Selecting Nonconsecutive Files

To select multiple files whose names are not consecutive, follow these steps:

 Hold down the Ctrl key, and click on each filename you desire.

1. Move the selection frame to the first file and press Shift+F8. The selection frame begins to blink.

2. Use the arrow keys and the Spacebar to select each file you desire.

3. After you select all the files you want, press Shift+F8.

Selecting All Files

To select all the files in the contents pane, click on a file in the contents pane or move the selection frame to the contents pane, and then press Ctrl+/.

Selecting or Deselecting Files by Pattern

To select files that match a pattern, follow these steps:

1. Choose Select Files from the File menu. A dialog box similar to the one shown in Figure 2-16 appears.

FIGURE 2-16. *The Select Files dialog box.*

2. Type in the wildcard pattern that corresponds to the files you want to select. (For more information about pattern matching, see your MS-DOS manual.)

3. To select the files that match your pattern, choose the Select button. To deselect the files that match your pattern, choose the Deselect button.

Canceling a Selection

To cancel a selection, follow these steps:

Hold down the Ctrl key, and click on the file to deselect it.

1. Move the selection frame to the contents pane, and then press Shift+F8. The selection frame begins to blink.

2. Use the arrow keys to move the selection frame to the file you want to deselect. Press the Spacebar.

3. Press Shift+F8.

Canceling All Selections

To cancel all file selections, click on a file in the contents pane, or move the selection frame to the contents pane and press Ctrl+\.

Using the File Menu

The File menu performs a variety of tasks, such as renaming and copying files. Figure 2-17 briefly describes each File command.

Command	Function
Open	Runs the selected application, or runs the application that created the selected document and loads the document into the application
Move	Moves one or more files to a different disk or directory
Copy	Copies one or more files to a different disk or directory
Delete	Deletes one or more files or directories
Rename	Renames one or more files
Properties	Assigns new file attributes to one or more selected files
Run	Runs an application
Print	Prints one or more files
Associate	Associates a file type (extension) with an application
Create Directory	Creates a directory
Search	Searches a disk for one or more files
Select Files	Selects files in the contents pane
Exit	Exits the File Manager

FIGURE 2-17. *File menu commands.*

Printing Files

To print one or more files, follow these steps:

1. Select the file or files you want to print.

2. Choose Print from the File menu. A dialog box similar to the one in Figure 2-18 appears.

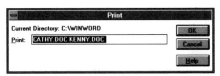

FIGURE 2-18. *The Print dialog box.*

3. Choose OK.

TIP: *If the Print Manager is running, a quick way to print a file is to drag the file's icon on top of the Print Manager icon.*

NOTE: *A document must be associated with an application before it can be printed from the File Manager.*

Associating Files

Every document file created with a Windows-based application has a *filename extension.* (For example, every Write document file has the

WRI filename extension.) This extension—the characters at the end of the filename—can be *associated* with an application.

By associating an extension with an application, you can have Windows run the associated application—and load the selected file—each time you choose a file with that file extension. (For example, by simply choosing any file with the WRI extension, you'd trigger Write to begin and load the file you chose.)

To associate a filename extension with an application, follow these steps:

1. Select a file with the desired filename extension from a directory window.

2. Choose Associate from the File menu. A dialog box similar to the one shown in Figure 2-19 appears.

FIGURE 2-19. *The Associate dialog box.*

3. If the application you desire is in the Associate With list box, select the application.

4. If the Associate With list box does not contain the application you desire, choose Browse. A dialog box similar to the one shown in Figure 2-20 appears.

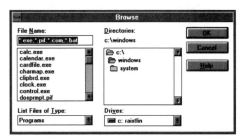

FIGURE 2-20. *The Browse dialog box.*

5. Choose the application's drive in the Drives drop-down list box, and the application's directory in the Directories list box. Select the application in the list box.

6. Choose OK. The Browse dialog box closes, and the appropriate information is added to the Associate dialog box. Choose OK.

Searching Your Disk for a File

If you can't locate a file, you can use the File Manager to search for it. The File Manager opens a window containing a list of each matching file.

To search for a file, follow these steps:

1. Choose Search from the File menu. A dialog box similar to the one shown in Figure 2-21 appears.

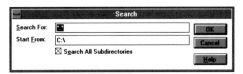

FIGURE 2-21. *The Search dialog box.*

2. Type the name of the file (or pattern) you want to search for into the Search For text box.

3. Type the name of the directory you want the File Manager to search into the Start From text box.

4. Select the Search All Subdirectories check box if you want the File Manager to search the subdirectories of the specified directory. Otherwise, the File Manager searches only the specified directory. Choose OK. If the File Manager locates one or more matching files, it opens a window listing the files, as shown in Figure 2-22.

FIGURE 2-22. *The Search Results window.*

Moving Files and Directories

To move files and directories, follow these steps:

1. Open a directory window that displays the files and directories you want to move. Open a directory window that displays the directory to which you want to move the files and directories. Make a portion of both windows visible.

2. Select the files and directories you want to move.

3. Drag the files and directories into the new directory window.

4. If the File Manager displays a dialog box asking you to confirm the move, choose Yes.

1. Select the files and directories you want to move.

2. Choose Move from the File menu, or press F7. A dialog box similar to the one shown in Figure 2-23 appears.

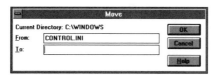

FIGURE 2-23. *The Move dialog box.*

3. Type in the pathname of the directory to which you want the files and directories moved. Choose OK.

Copying Files and Directories

To copy files and directories, follow these steps:

1. Open a directory window that displays the files and directories you want to copy. Open a second directory window that displays the directory to which you want to copy the files and directories. Make a portion of both windows visible.

2. Select the files and directories to copy.

3. Hold down the Ctrl key, and drag the selected files and directories into the new window.

4. If the File Manager displays a dialog box asking you to confirm the copy, choose Yes.

1. Select the files and directories you want to copy.

2. Choose Copy from the File menu, or press F8. A dialog box similar to the one shown in Figure 2-24 appears.

3. Type in the pathname of the directory to which you want the files and directories copied.

4. If you'd like to create a link to the file that can be embedded in an application, select the Copy to Clipboard radio button. (For more information on embedding, see the

section on the Object Packager in Part IV, "Desktop Applications.")

5. Choose OK.

FIGURE 2-24. *The Copy dialog box.*

Deleting a File or Directory

The File Manager lets you delete both files and directories. Note that when you delete a directory, all files and subdirectories in that directory are also deleted.

To delete a file or directory, follow these steps:

1. Select the file or directory you want to delete.

2. Choose Delete from the File menu, or press the Delete key. A dialog box similar to the one shown in Figure 2-25 appears.

FIGURE 2-25. *The Delete dialog box.*

3. Choose OK.

4. If the File Manager displays a dialog box asking you to confirm the deletion, choose Yes.

Adding an Item to a Group Window

File Manager offers a convenient way of adding an application or a document to a group window. Simply drag the desired icon from File Manager into the group window where you want to add the application or document.

Renaming a File or Directory

To rename a file or directory, follow these steps:

1. Select the file or directory to rename.

2. Choose Rename from the File menu. A dialog box similar to the one shown in Figure 2-26 appears.

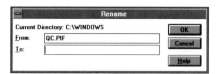

FIGURE 2-26. *The Rename dialog box.*

3. Type in the new name. Choose OK.

Assigning File Attributes

The File Manager lets you assign new file attributes to one or more files. The following list describes the available attributes:

File Attribute	Meaning
Read Only	Prevents the file from being changed or deleted
Archive	Identifies the file as needing to be backed up
Hidden	Prevents the file from appearing in an MS-DOS directory list
System	Identifies a special MS-DOS system file

To assign file attributes to one or more files, follow these steps:

1. Select the desired files.

2. Choose Properties from the File menu. A dialog box similar to the one shown in Figure 2-27 appears.

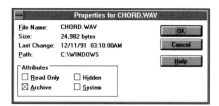

FIGURE 2-27. *The Properties dialog box.*

3. Select a check box to assign the associated attribute, or deselect the check box to remove the associated attribute. Choose OK.

Using the Disk Menu

The Disk menu lets you copy, label, and format disks, as well as connect to network drives. The following list describes the commands available on the Disk menu.

Command	Function
Copy Disk	Copies the contents of one floppy disk to another
Label Disk	Assigns a volume label to a disk

(continued)

continued

Command	Function
Format Disk	Formats a floppy disk
Make System Disk	Makes a disk a boot disk
Network Connections	Connects or disconnects your computer to or from a network drive
Select Drive	Changes the currently selected drive to another drive

Copying One Floppy Disk to Another

The File Manager lets you copy the contents of one floppy disk to a second floppy disk of identical size and capacity. The disk copy operation overwrites the contents of the second disk. If the second floppy disk is not formatted, the File Manager formats it for you.

To copy one floppy disk (called the *source disk*) to another floppy disk (called the *destination disk*), follow these steps:

1. Insert the source disk into a disk drive. If you have dual disk drives of the same size and capacity, insert the destination disk into the second disk drive.

2. Choose Copy Disk from the Disk menu. The dialog box shown in Figure 2-28 appears.

FIGURE 2-28. *The Copy Disk dialog box.*

3. Choose the drive letter of the source disk from the Source In drop-down list box.

4. Choose the drive letter of the destination disk from the Destination In drop-down list box. (On single floppy-disk drive systems, the source and destination drives are the same.) Choose OK.

5. A dialog box appears, asking you to confirm the copy operation. Choose Yes.

Labeling a Disk

A volume label is an 11-character name you can assign to a disk to improve your disk organization. To assign a volume label to a disk, follow these steps:

1. Select the drive containing the disk you want to label.

2. Choose Label Disk from the Disk menu. A dialog box similar to the one shown in Figure 2-29 appears, containing the existing volume label, if the disk has one.

FIGURE 2-29. *The Label Disk dialog box.*

3. Type in the volume label name you desire, and choose OK.

Formatting a Floppy Disk

To format a floppy disk with the File Manager, follow these steps:

1. Insert the floppy disk into a drive.

2. Choose Format Disk from the Disk menu. A dialog box similar to the one shown in Figure 2-30 appears.

FIGURE 2-30. *The Format Disk dialog box.*

3. If necessary, select the drive the disk resides in from the Disk In drop-down list.

4. If necessary, select the disk's size in the Capacity drop-down list.

5. If you want to assign a volume label to the disk, select the Label text box and type in an 11-character volume name.

6. If you want the disk to be bootable, select the Make System Disk check box.

7. If you want to reformat a previously formatted disk, select the Quick Format check box. A quick format creates a new file allocation table and root directory, but the disk is not scanned for bad areas. A quick format is much faster than a normal format, but use this option only on disks that you know to have no errors.

8. Choose OK.

9. If the File Manager displays a dialog box asking you to confirm the format operation, choose Yes.

Creating a System Disk

Before you can boot MS-DOS from a disk, the disk must contain special system files. To copy the system files to a floppy disk, follow these steps:

1. Choose Make System Disk from the Disk menu. A dialog box similar to the one shown in Figure 2-31 appears.

FIGURE 2-31. *The Make System Disk dialog box.*

2. Choose the disk to which you want to copy the system files.

3. Choose OK.

Connecting to a Network Drive

If your computer is connected to a network, your computer can connect to network drives. (A network drive is a shared drive on another computer that is also connected to the network.) To connect your computer to a network drive, follow these steps:

1. Choose Network Connections from the Disk menu. A dialog box similar to the one shown in Figure 2-32 appears.

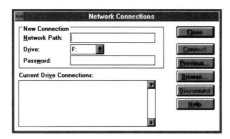

FIGURE 2-32. *The Network Connections dialog box.*

2. Type in the network pathname required to locate the drive, or select a previously connected pathname using the Previous button.

   NOTE: *If you're not sure of the network pathname, you might be able to use the Browse button to view available network drives.*

3. Select a drive letter for the network drive.

4. Type in the drive's password, if required.

5. Choose Connect.

6. Choose Close.

Disconnecting from a Network Drive

To disconnect from a network drive, follow these steps:

1. Choose Network Connections from the Disk menu. A dialog box similar to the one shown in Figure 2-33 appears.

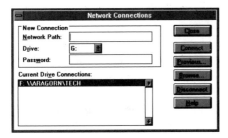

FIGURE 2-33. *The Network Connections dialog box.*

2. Select the drive you want to disconnect from the Current Drive Connections list box.

3. Choose Disconnect.

4. Choose Close.

Determining the Amount of Available Memory

To determine the amount of available memory on your system, choose About from the Help menu. A dialog box appears similar to the one shown in Figure 2-34, displaying information about Windows and the amount of available memory.

FIGURE 2-34. *The About File Manager dialog box.*

Controlling Confirmation Dialog Boxes

By default, the File Manager displays a dialog box confirming several operations, such as replacement and deletion of files. You can control whether these confirmation dialog boxes appear by using the Options menu. The following list describes the available confirmations:

Confirmation	Action
File Delete	A warning before deleting files
Directory Delete	A warning before deleting a subdirectory
File Replace	A warning before overwriting an existing file
Mouse Action	A warning before copying or moving files dragged by a mouse
Disk Commands	A warning before formatting or copying a disk

To enable or disable one or more confirmations, follow these steps:

1. Choose Confirmation from the Options menu. A dialog box similar to the one shown in Figure 2-35 appears.

FIGURE 2-35. *The Confirmation dialog box.*

2. Select a check box to enable confirmation of that operation. Deselect the check box to turn confirmation off. Choose OK when you're satisfied with the confirmation settings.

Selecting a File Manager Font

The File Manager lets you select the font used to display file and directory names. To select a font, follow these steps:

1. Choose Font from the Options menu. A dialog box similar to the one shown in Figure 2-36 appears.

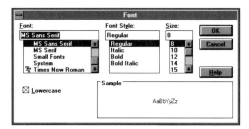

FIGURE 2-36. *The Font dialog box.*

2. Select a font from the Font list box. The Sample box shows several letters drawn in the font you've selected.

3. Select a font style from the Font Style list box. The Sample box shows several letters drawn in the font style you've selected.

4. Select a font size from the Size list box. The Sample box shows several letters drawn in the font size you've selected.

5. If you prefer to see file and directory names in lowercase letters, select the Lowercase check box; otherwise, deselect the Lowercase check box.

6. Choose OK.

Other File Manager Options

By using the Options menu, you can customize the File Manager to your liking, as described in the following list. A check mark in front of a command on the screen means that the command is active.

Command	Function
Status Bar	Controls whether the status bar appears at the bottom of the File Manager window
Minimize on Use	Controls whether the File Manager is minimized when you start another application from the File Manager
Save Settings on Exit	Saves the positions of open directory windows when you exit the File Manager

Exiting the File Manager

To exit the File Manager, double-click on the File Manager's Control menu box, or choose Exit from the File menu.

THE CLIPBOARD VIEWER

Windows uses the *Clipboard*—a temporary storage area in memory—to let you exchange information (either text or graphics) between applications. Information is copied to the Clipboard from one application, and then copied from the Clipboard and pasted into the second application. The Clipboard Viewer lets you save Clipboard files, open Clipboard files, or clear the Clipboard.

Saving Clipboard Files

To save the information on the Clipboard, follow these steps:

1. Choose Save As from the File menu. A dialog box similar to the one shown in Figure 2-37 appears.

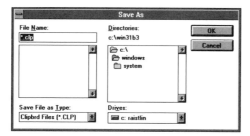

FIGURE 2-37. *The Save As dialog box.*

2. Type the name of the file to which the information is to be saved. Use the Drives drop-down list and the Directories list box to choose the file's drive and subdirectory.

3. Choose OK.

Opening Clipboard Files

To open a Clipboard file, follow these steps:

1. Choose Open from the File menu. A dialog box similar to the one shown in Figure 2-38 appears.

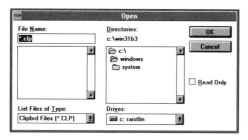

FIGURE 2-38. *The Open dialog box.*

2. Use the Drives drop-down list and the Directories list box to choose the file's drive and subdirectory, and then select the file in the File Name list box.

3. Choose OK.

Clearing the Clipboard

To clear the Clipboard, choose Delete from the Edit menu, or press the Delete key. Windows asks whether you want to clear the Clipboard. Choose Yes to clear the Clipboard, or No to leave the information on the Clipboard.

THE PRINT MANAGER

When you print from a Windows-based application, the application sends the print file to the Print Manager. The Print Manager works in the background, sending files to the printer while you continue working. As you send files to the Print Manager, it forms a print queue—a list of files waiting to be printed.

NOTE: *When you install Windows, Setup lets you identify and configure one or more printers. If you later add or change a printer, choose the Control Panel icon from the Program Manager window, and then choose the Printers icon to inform Windows of the change.*

There are actually two types of print queues: *local* and *network*. A local queue is a list of files waiting to be sent to a printer attached to your computer, whereas a network queue is a list of files waiting to be printed on a network printer.

When you send files to a local queue, the Print Manager icon appears at the bottom of your desktop. By choosing this icon, you can view, rearrange, or delete files in the local print queue, as well as set several options that control how the Print Manager behaves. (Most networks, however, don't allow you to perform these functions on a network queue.)

Viewing Queued Files

To view the names of the files in the print queue, choose the Print Manager icon. The Print Manager window—similar to Figure 2-39—appears on your screen.

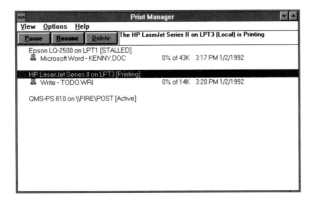

FIGURE 2-39. *The Print Manager window.*

If your computer has multiple printers or is attached to a network printer, information appears about each printer's queue.

Displaying Size, Time, and Date Information

By default, the Print Manager displays each file's size and the time and date you sent the file to be printed. To toggle this information on and off, choose Print File Size and Time/Date Sent from the View menu. A check mark in front of a command on the screen means the command is active.

Viewing Network Print Queues

By default, the Print Manager displays the names of only those files that you have sent to the network print queue. To view all files in a network queue, select the queue and choose Selected Net Queue from the View menu. A dialog box appears—similar to Figure 2-40—listing all files in the network queue.

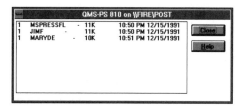

FIGURE 2-40. *A list of files in the network queue.*

Viewing Other Network Queues

With some networks, the Print Manager lets you view network print queues for other printers connected to the network. To view the print queue for a network printer your computer is not connected to, follow these steps:

1. Choose Other Net Queue from the View menu.

2. When the dialog box appears, type the desired queue name and choose View.

3. Choose Close after you finish.

Network Queue Status

Print Manager automatically updates the status of network queues periodically. Print Manager also lets you manually update the queue status. To manually update the queue status, choose Refresh from the View menu, or press F5.

Changing the Print Queue Order

To change the position of a file in a print queue, follow these steps:

Drag the filename to its new position.

Select the filename, and move it to its new position using Ctrl+Up arrow or Ctrl+Down arrow.

Removing Files from the Print Queue

To remove a file from the print queue, select its filename, and then choose Delete. The Print Manager displays a dialog box to confirm the deletion.

NOTE: *Your network might not allow you to remove files from a network queue.*

Controlling the Print Manager's Priority

The Print Manager works as a background task, printing files at the same time you are running other applications. To do this, your computer spends some time running applications and some time printing files. Use the Options menu to set the Print Manager's *priority,* which controls how much time your computer spends printing files. The following list describes the priority possibilities:

Command	Result
Low Priority	Your computer spends more time running applications than printing files. Applications run quickly, but files take a long time to print
Medium Priority	Your computer spends an equal amount of time running applications and printing files. This is the default setting
High Priority	Your computer spends more time printing files than running applications. Files print quickly, but applications might be sluggish

Pausing and Resuming Printing

At times you might need to temporarily stop a local queue from printing files. (Most network software does not let you stop a network queue from printing files.) Using the Print Manager's Pause and Resume buttons, you can temporarily stop and later restart a queue printing files.

Pausing Printing

To temporarily stop a queue from printing files, follow these steps:

1. Select the queue.

2. Choose the Pause button.

Resuming Printing

To resume printing from a queue, follow these steps:

1. Select the queue.

2. Choose the Resume button.

Handling Printing Problems

Because it operates in the background, the Print Manager needs a way to let you know when something goes wrong (when the printer is out of paper, for example). The Options menu lets you specify how the Print Manager is to provide such information. The following list describes the possibilities.

Command	Result
Always Alert	Print Manager immediately displays a message dialog box
Flash if Inactive	Print Manager beeps once and then flashes the Print Manager title bar or icon until you enlarge the Print Manager icon or select the Print Manager window
Ignore if Inactive	Print Manager ignores the problem. (The printer status is changed to *stalled*)

Other Network Options

You control whether the Print Manager automatically updates its display for network queues and whether print jobs sent to a network queue bypass the Print Manager. To change one of these options, follow these steps:

1. Choose Network Settings from the Options menu. A dialog box similar to the one shown in Figure 2-41 appears.

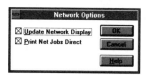

FIGURE 2-41. *The Network Options dialog box.*

2. Select the Update Network Display check box if you want the Print
   Manager to automatically update the display for network queues.

3. Select Print Net Jobs Direct if you want applications to bypass the
   Print Manager and send documents directly to a network printer (this
   speeds up some print jobs).

4. Choose OK.

Closing the Print Manager

To close the Print Manager, double-click on the Control menu box or
choose Exit from the Options menu. Closing the Print Manager deletes
all files in all print queues, so the Print Manager displays a dialog box
asking you to confirm the deletions.

THE TASK LIST

Windows lets you run several applications at the same time, each within
its own window. To move among these windows quickly, you can either
click in a window or use the Task List.

Activating the Task List

To activate the Task List, double-click your mouse anywhere on the
desktop (outside of windows and away from icons), or press Ctrl+Esc. A
dialog box similar to the one shown in Figure 2-42 appears.

FIGURE 2-42. *The Task List dialog box.*

Using the Task List

To switch to an application, simply double-click on the desired application name, or use the arrow keys to select the application name and then
choose Switch To.

Stopping Applications with the Task List

You can also use the Task List to stop applications. Simply select the name of the application, and choose End Task. If the application has open documents, Windows prompts you to save the changes.

Canceling the Task List

After you finish using the Task List, click on Cancel or press Esc.

THE PIF EDITOR

The more Windows knows about the way a program operates, the better Windows integrates that application into the Windows environment with the rest of your applications. Applications designed for Windows automatically supply Windows with the information it needs, but applications not designed for Windows (such as MS-DOS–based applications) do not.

A *PIF* is a Program Information File that provides Windows with key information it needs to know about applications not designed for Windows. In most cases, you don't need to create a PIF for all of these types of applications you use; Windows provides a default PIF that is normally sufficient. If you want to provide Windows with more specific information about an application not designed for Windows, however, you can create a PIF using the PIF Editor. Depending on the mode, the steps you perform—and the information you provide—differ. In either mode, however, you perform the following operations.

Creating a PIF

To create a PIF for an application not designed for Windows, follow these steps:

1. Expand the PIF Editor icon in the Main group window.

2. Set all fields as desired. (Standard mode fields are covered in the section titled "Standard Mode" below. 386 Enhanced mode fields are covered in the section titled "386 Enhanced Mode" below.)

3. After you complete all fields, choose Save As from the File menu. Type in a filename, and choose OK.

Editing an Existing PIF

To edit an existing PIF, follow these steps:

1. Choose Open from the File menu.

2. Type in the name of the file, or select the file using the File Name and Directories list boxes.

3. Set all fields as desired. (Standard mode fields are covered in the section below titled "Standard Mode." 386 Enhanced mode fields are covered in the section below titled "386 Enhanced Mode.")

4. Choose Save from the File menu.

Standard Mode

When you run the PIF Editor in standard mode, a PIF Editor window similar to the one shown in Figure 2-43 appears.

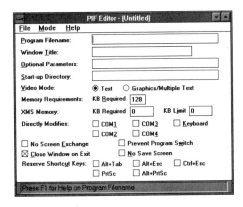

FIGURE 2-43. *A PIF Editor window.*

The following paragraphs briefly describe each standard mode PIF field:

■ *Program Filename* specifies the application's complete pathname (drive, directory, filename, and extension). If the application is in your computer's search path (as listed in your computer's AUTOEXEC.BAT file), you need only enter the application's name and extension.

■ *Window Title* specifies the name you want to appear in the application's title bar or beneath the application's icon when minimized. Typically, you use the application's name.

- *Optional Parameters* specifies the application's command line. If you use the question mark (?), Windows displays a dialog box before the application runs to prompt you for the parameters.

- *Start-up Directory* directs Windows to change to the directory specified before running the application. If you don't specify a directory, Windows uses the application's directory.

- *Video Mode* specifies the video mode in which the application runs. If you are not sure of the video mode used, select Graphics/Multiple Text.

- *Memory Requirements* tells Windows the minimum amount of conventional memory (in KB) the application needs.

- *XMS Memory* has two fields: KB Required and KB Limit. KB Required specifies the amount of extended memory (in KB) the application needs. KB Limit specifies the maximum amount of extended memory Windows lets the application use.

- *Directly Modifies* tells Windows what devices the application modifies, letting Windows restrict the device's use by other applications.

- *No Screen Exchange* prevents you from copying the application's screen into the Clipboard using Print Screen and Alt+Print Screen. The only reason to select this option is to provide a small amount of extra memory to the application.

- *Prevent Program Switch* lets Windows save a small amount of memory by preventing you from switching from this application to another. When this option is selected, you exit the application to return to Windows.

- *Close Window on Exit* directs Windows to close the application's window when the application ends, as opposed to displaying the application's ending screen and prompting you with the message *Hit Any Key to Exit.*

- *No Save Screen* directs Windows not to save a copy of a program designed for MS-DOS's screen when you switch to another application. The application's screen might not be restored correctly when you return to it.

- *Reserve Shortcut Keys* directs Windows to reserve the specified keyboard combinations for the application's use, instead of treating the keys as predefined Windows keyboard combinations.

386 Enhanced Mode

When you run the PIF Editor in 386 Enhanced mode, a PIF Editor window similar to the one shown in Figure 2-44 appears.

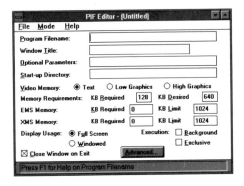

FIGURE 2-44. *A PIF Editor window.*

The following paragraphs briefly describe each 386 Enhanced mode PIF field:

■ *Program Filename* specifies the application's complete pathname (drive, directory, filename, and extension). If the application is in your computer's search path (as listed in your computer's AUTOEXEC.BAT file), you need only enter the application's name and extension.

■ *Window Title* specifies the name you want to appear in the application's title bar or beneath the application's icon when minimized. Typically, you use the application's name.

■ *Optional Parameters* specifies the application's command line. If you use the question mark (?), Windows displays a dialog box before the application runs to prompt you for the parameters.

■ *Start-up Directory* directs Windows to change to the directory specified before running the application. If you don't specify a directory, Windows uses the application's directory.

■ *Video Memory* specifies how much memory Windows reserves to save the application's window when it switches between tasks. If the application uses text mode, select Text. If the application uses CGA graphics, select Low Graphics. If the application uses EGA or VGA graphics, select High Graphics.

■ *Memory Requirements* has two fields: KB Required and KB Desired. KB Required specifies the minimum amount of conventional memory the application needs. KB Desired specifies the maximum amount of conventional memory Windows lets the application use. The only reason to change this entry is to reserve more memory for other applications.

- *EMS Memory* has two fields: KB Required and KB Limit. KB Required specifies the minimum amount of expanded memory the application needs. KB Limit specifies the maximum amount of expanded memory Windows lets the application use.

- *XMS Memory* has two fields: KB Required and KB Limit. KB Required specifies the minimum amount of extended memory the application needs. KB Limit specifies the maximum amount of extended memory Windows lets the application use.

- *Display Usage* has two option buttons: Full Screen and Windowed. Full Screen specifies that the application runs full screen, while Windowed specifies that the application runs in a window. Windows lets you toggle the display of an application not designed for Windows between full screen and a window by pressing Alt+Enter.

- *Execution* contains two check boxes: Background and Exclusive. If you select Background, Windows allows the application to run in the background while you use another application. If you deselect Background, Windows stops running the application when you switch to another application. Selecting Exclusive tells Windows to suspend execution of all other applications while the application controlled by this PIF is running in the foreground—even if the other applications have their Background option selected. The advantage of this option is that the application controlled by this PIF runs faster and has access to more memory.

- *Close Window on Exit* directs Windows to close the application's window when the application ends, as opposed to displaying the application's ending screen and prompting you with the message *Hit Any Key to Exit*.

At the bottom of the dialog box is a button labeled Advanced. Choosing Advanced brings up a second dialog box, similar to the one shown in Figure 2-45.

The following paragraphs briefly describe the fields in this dialog box:

- *Background Priority* and *Foreground Priority* control the amount of time Windows spends running the application when the application is running in the background or in the foreground. Priority values range from 0 through 10,000. These values are meaningful only when compared to other applications.

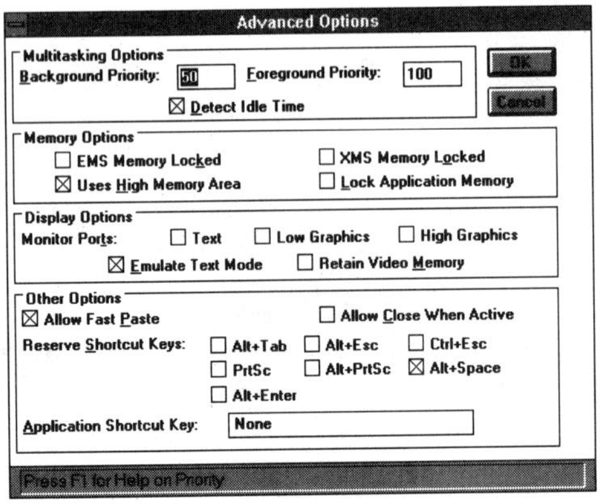

FIGURE 2-45. *The Advanced Options dialog box.*

For example, suppose three applications are running. The application in the foreground has a foreground priority of 100, and the two applications in the background have a background priority of 50. Therefore, the total priority for all applications is 200. Windows spends a percentage of time running each application equal to the application's priority divided by the total priority of all applications. Therefore, the foreground application is running 50 percent of the time (100 ÷ 200), and each background application is running 25 percent of the time (50 ÷ 200).

■ *Detect Idle Time* directs Windows to let other applications run while an application is idle, waiting for your input.

■ *EMS Memory Locked* prevents Windows from swapping the contents of the application's expanded memory to disk. This increases the application's performance but decreases overall Windows performance.

■ *XMS Memory Locked* prevents Windows from swapping the contents of the application's extended memory to disk. This increases the application's performance but decreases overall Windows performance.

■ *Uses High Memory Area* tells Windows that the application can use the high memory area (the first 64 KB of extended memory).

■ *Lock Application Memory* prevents Windows from swapping the program to disk. This increases the application's performance but decreases overall Windows performance.

■ The *Monitor Ports* check boxes help prevent problems that can occur when an application directly interacts with your computer's display adaptor. If your application's display looks normal, don't modify these settings because they slow down the application significantly.

Otherwise, select the option button that corresponds to the video mode the application runs in (Text for text mode, Low Graphics for CGA graphics mode, and High Graphics for EGA or VGA graphics mode).

■ *Emulate Text Mode* lets Windows quickly display an application's text output. Leave this option selected unless the application's display doesn't appear properly.

■ *Retain Video Memory* directs Windows not to reduce the amount of memory used for an application's display when the application is running. This prevents the application from losing video memory when you switch to another graphics mode.

■ *Allow Fast Paste* lets Windows paste text from the clipboard into the application as fast as possible. If an application has difficulties with paste operations, disable this option.

■ *Allow Close When Active* allows Windows to close an active application automatically when you exit Windows.

■ *Reserve Shortcut Keys* directs Windows to reserve the specified key combinations for use by the application instead of treating the key combinations as predefined Windows shortcut keys.

■ *Application Shortcut Key* lets you specify a shortcut key that makes the application the foreground task.

PART III

Customizing and Optimizing Windows with the Control Panel

Windows lets you customize several features, ensuring that your computer does the best possible job of suiting your needs and providing a comfortable working environment. In this section, you learn to take advantage of the versatility Windows offers.

At the heart of Windows customization is the *Control Panel.* The Control Panel provides you with a variety of options that let you set up Windows in the way that works best for you.

To use the Control Panel, expand the Control Panel icon from the Program Manager window. The window shown in Figure 3-1 appears.

Control Panel options appear as icons within the Control Panel window. These options perform the following tasks:

Change screen colors (*Color*)

Manage fonts (*Fonts*)

Configure serial ports (*Ports*)

Customize mouse (*Mouse*)

Customize desktop (*Desktop*)

Set keyboard response (*Keyboard*)

Configure printers (*Printers*)

Specify international settings (*International*)

Set date and time (*Date/Time*)

Set network options (*Network*)

Select MIDI setup for sound device (*MIDI Mapper*)

Specify which applications have priority (*386 Enhanced*)

Install drivers for sound cards and CD-ROMs (*Drivers*)

Disable warning beeps (*Sound*)

Windows displays explanatory text at the bottom of the Control Panel window that describes the current option. If you click on an option or select an option using the arrow keys, Windows displays explanatory text for that option. The following sections describe how to use each of the Control Panel's options.

FIGURE 3-1. *The Control Panel and its options.*

CHANGING SCREEN COLORS

The Color option lets you change the colors used for different areas of the screen, such as the desktop, window background, window borders, window title bar, and so on. When you choose the Color option, a dialog box similar to the one shown in Figure 3-2 appears.

FIGURE 3-2. *The Color dialog box.*

This dialog box represents the different areas of your desktop—windows, window borders, title bars, and so on. As you select different colors, you see how the colors actually appear on your screen by looking at the model of the screen inside the dialog box.

Using a Predefined Color Scheme

Windows comes with several predefined color combinations. To use a predefined color combination, follow these steps:

1. Open the Color Schemes drop-down list box.

2. Select a color scheme from the list. The colors in the dialog box change to reflect your selection.

3. When you see a color scheme you like, choose OK. Windows adopts the new color scheme.

Changing the Color of a Desktop Element

To change the color of a particular screen element, such as window title bars or scroll bars, follow these steps:

1. Choose Color Palette >>. A dialog box similar to the one shown in Figure 3-3 appears.

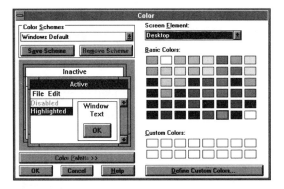

FIGURE 3-3. *The Color dialog box with palette.*

2. Open the Screen Element drop-down list box, and select the screen element whose color you want to change.

3. Select the new color, and choose OK.

Creating a Color

The Color application also lets you create your own colors. To do so, follow these steps:

1. Move to the Custom Colors field, and select a box for the new color.

2. Choose Define Custom Colors. A dialog box similar to the one shown in Figure 3-4 appears.

3. Select the color you want by following these steps:

 Click within the Custom Color Selector to move the cross hairs to the desired color scheme. Then adjust the brightness of the color by dragging the luminosity arrow at the right of the Custom Color Selector. The Color|Solid box reflects your current selection.

Cross hairs

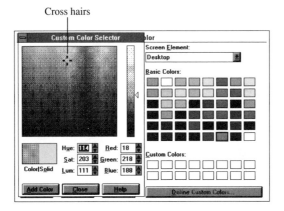

FIGURE 3-4. *The Custom Color Selector dialog box.*

 Move to the boxes beneath the Custom Color Selector, and specify a value for each. Valid values are as follows: Hue, 0 through 239; Sat(uration) and Lum(inosity), 0 through 240; Red, Green, and Blue, 0 through 255. The Color|Solid box reflects your current selection.

The following diagram shows how these numbers are interpreted in the Custom Color Selector:

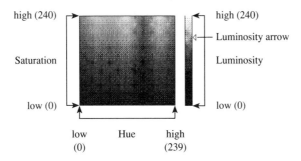

4. Choose Add Color.

5. Choose Close.

MANAGING FONTS

A *font* is a complete set of typographic characters of a certain size. A *font file* is a file that contains a font. When you purchase a new font file, you add it to Windows so that you can use it. When you choose the Fonts icon in the Control Panel window, a dialog box similar to the one shown in Figure 3-5 appears.

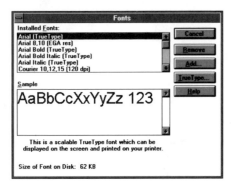

FIGURE 3-5. *The Fonts dialog box.*

Adding a Font

To add a font, follow these steps:

1. Choose Fonts from the Control Panel window.

2. Choose Add. A dialog box similar to the one shown in Figure 3-6 appears.

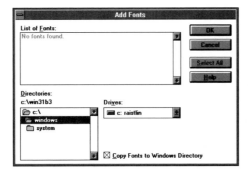

FIGURE 3-6. *The Add Fonts dialog box.*

3. Open the Drives drop-down list and select the drive that contains the font file.

4. Open the Directories drop-down list and select the directory containing the font file.

5. Select the font in the List of Fonts list box.

6. Choose OK.

Removing a Font

To remove a font, follow these steps:

1. Choose Fonts from the Control Panel window.

2. From the Installed Fonts list box, select the font you want to remove.

3. Choose Remove.

4. A second dialog box appears asking you to confirm the font removal. Choose Yes to remove the font, or choose No to cancel the procedure.

Using TrueType Fonts

A TrueType font is a sizable font that prints exactly as it appears on your screen. You can control whether Windows uses TrueType fonts, and whether it uses them exclusively. To use TrueType fonts, follow these steps:

1. Choose TrueType in the Fonts dialog box. The TrueType dialog box similar to the one shown in Figure 3-7 appears.

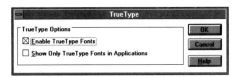

FIGURE 3-7. *The TrueType dialog box.*

2. Select the Enable TrueType Fonts check box to let Windows use TrueType fonts.

3. Select the Show Only TrueType Fonts in Applications check box to make Windows use only TrueType fonts.

4. Choose OK.

CONFIGURING SERIAL PORTS

Serial ports let you connect a mouse, modem, or other hardware device to your computer. As part of the connection process, you set the communication parameters of each serial port to match the parameters of the device. (The manual for your hardware device describes its parameters.) To do so, expand the Ports icon from the Control Panel window. The dialog box shown in Figure 3-8 appears.

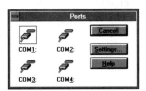

FIGURE 3-8. *The Ports dialog box.*

To set a port's communication parameters, follow these steps:

1. Select the desired port.

2. Choose Settings. A dialog box similar to the one shown in Figure 3-9 appears.

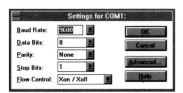

FIGURE 3-9. *The Settings dialog box.*

3. Open the Baud Rate drop-down list box and select the desired baud rate.

4. Open the Data Bits drop-down list box and select the desired number of data bits.

5. Open the Parity drop-down list box and select the desired parity.

6. Open the Stop Bits drop-down list box and select the desired number of stop bits.

7. Open the Flow Control drop-down list box and select the desired method of flow control.

8. After you finish setting the port's communication parameters, choose OK. Choose Close in the Ports dialog box.

Communications Terminology

If you're going to set up ports, you need to be familiar with the following terms in the Ports dialog box:

Baud rate The speed with which information is transferred through the port.

Data bits The number of data bits used for each character.

Parity The method of error-checking that both devices agree to use.

Stop bits The amount of time between transmitted characters (one stop bit is the time necessary to transmit one bit).

Flow control The method used to control the flow of data.

CUSTOMIZING THE MOUSE

If you have a mouse, you can use the Control Panel's Mouse icon to control how fast the mouse pointer moves and how fast you double-click to choose items. You can even swap the actions of the left and right mouse buttons (a handy option for left-handed mouse users).

To customize your mouse, expand the Mouse icon from the Control Panel window. A dialog box similar to the one shown in Figure 3-10 appears.

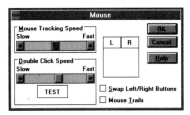

FIGURE 3-10. *The Mouse dialog box.*

Setting Mouse Tracking Speed

To set mouse tracking speed (the speed at which the mouse cursor moves across the screen), simply drag the Mouse Tracking Speed scroll box to the desired area in the scroll bar.

Setting Double-Click Speed

To set the double-click speed, simply drag the Double-Click Speed scroll box to the desired area in the scroll bar. To test the double-click speed, double-click on the box labeled *TEST*. If the box changes color, your double-click was fast enough to choose an item.

Swapping Left/Right Buttons

To swap the functions of the left and right mouse buttons (helpful if you're a lefty), select the Swap Left/Right Buttons check box.

Selecting Mouse Trails

The Mouse Trails option improves the visibility of the mouse pointer on LCD screens. Selecting the Mouse Trails option changes your mouse pointer from a single arrow to a collection of arrows resembling an accordian that chases your mouse pointer across the screen. When you stop the pointer's movement, the trailing arrows catch up and merge to create a single arrow.

Choose OK after you finish customizing your mouse.

CUSTOMIZING YOUR DESKTOP

The default Windows desktop, while fully functional, is rather impersonal. You can, however, change the look of the desktop, the width of window borders, the cursor blink rate, and other items. To do so, expand the Desktop icon from the Control Panel window. A dialog box similar to the one shown in Figure 3-11 appears.

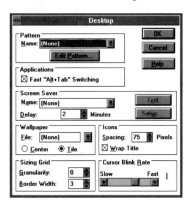

FIGURE 3-11. *The Desktop dialog box.*

Selecting a Background Pattern

By default, your desktop is a solid color. You can change the desktop to a predefined background pattern, create your own background pattern, or even use a graphics file created by Paintbrush or a similar application.

Windows provides several predefined background patterns, as shown in Figure 3-12.

To use a predefined background pattern, follow these steps:

1. Open the Name drop-down list box.

2. Choose a background pattern.

3. Choose OK.

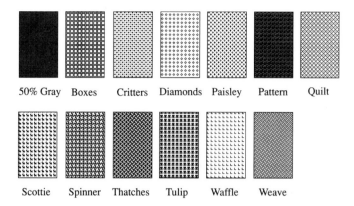

| 50% Gray | Boxes | Critters | Diamonds | Paisley | Pattern | Quilt |

| Scottie | Spinner | Thatches | Tulip | Waffle | Weave |

FIGURE 3-12. *Predefined background patterns.*

Creating Your Own Pattern

NOTE: *You need a mouse to create your own background pattern. You cannot create your own background pattern from the keyboard.*

If none of the predefined background patterns suit your tastes, you can create your own. To do so, follow these steps:

1. Choose Edit Pattern from the Pattern field. A dialog box similar to the one shown in Figure 3-13 appears.

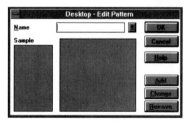

FIGURE 3-13. *The Desktop-Edit Pattern dialog box.*

2. Type in a name for your pattern, but do *not* press Enter.

3. Click inside the large center box. A large black square appears. Click on the square, and it disappears. The sample box shows what the pattern looks like on the desktop.

   □ To paint, click on a blank area and drag.

   □ To erase, click on a filled area and drag.

4. After you finish editing, choose Add.

5. Choose OK.

Editing an Existing Pattern

NOTE: *You need a mouse to edit a background pattern. You cannot edit a background pattern from the keyboard.*

To save time, you can also edit an existing background pattern. To do so, follow these steps:

1. Open the Name drop-down list box in the Desktop dialog box.

2. Select the pattern to edit.

3. Choose Edit Pattern in the Desktop dialog box.

4. Click inside the large center box. A large black square appears. Click on the square, and it disappears. The sample box shows what the pattern looks like on the desktop.

5. After you finish editing, choose Change.

6. Choose OK.

Deleting a Pattern

To delete a pattern, follow these steps:

1. Open the Name drop-down list box in the Desktop dialog box.

2. Select the pattern to remove.

3. Choose Edit Pattern in the Desktop dialog box.

4. Choose Remove.

5. A dialog box asks you to confirm the deletion. Choose Yes to remove the pattern, or choose No to cancel the procedure.

6. Choose OK.

Selecting Wallpaper

When it comes to customizing your desktop, you're not limited to background patterns. You can also use *wallpaper* (a graphics image) to add an interesting flair. Windows provides several predefined wallpapers, one of which is the Windows logo shown in Figure 3-14.

To select a wallpaper, follow these steps:

1. Open the File drop-down list box in the Desktop dialog box.

2. Select the desired wallpaper.

FIGURE 3-14. *One of several wallpapers available for use.*

3. Select either Center or Tile. Center centers the wallpaper on your desktop. Tile repeats the wallpaper as many times as necessary to completely cover your desktop.

NOTE: *The wallpaper does not appear until after you close the Desktop dialog box.*

4. Choose OK.

Using Fast Alt+Tab Switching

Fast Alt+Tab switching is a method of quickly switching between running applications. To enable Fast Alt+Tab switching, select the Fast Alt+Tab Switching check box in the Desktop dialog box.

To use Fast Alt+Tab switching, hold down the Alt key and press Tab (while continuing to hold down the Alt key). Windows draws a rectangle in the middle of the screen that contains the icon of a running application. Press Tab again (while still continuing to hold down the Alt key) and the icon of the next running application appears. Keep pressing Tab until you see the icon of the application to which you'd like to switch, and then release the Alt key.

Selecting a Screen Saver

Screen savers exist to prevent the monitor from permanently burning in a screen image, damaging your screen display. Usually, if the mouse is not moved and no keys are pressed for about two to five minutes, the user is not currently working with the system. During such periods, the screen-saver software begins displaying random or changing images. Windows provides several different screen savers, each of which displays a different image.

Screen Saver	Image
Blank Screen	Blanks the screen display
Marquee	Displays scrolling text on a blank background
Mystify	Displays random shapes created with a combination of lines
Starfield Simulation	Displays a simulation of flight through a starfield

To select a screen saver, open the drop-down list box and select the screen saver you want.

The Delay option lets you specify the amount of time that elapses without the mouse moving and no keys being pressed before the screen saver begins. To change the delay, click on the up or down arrow to increase or decrease the amount of time, or type in the desired delay, from 0 through 99 minutes.

Three of the screen savers—Marquee, Mystify, and Starfield Simulation—can be customized to suit your own taste.

Setting Up Marquee

To set up the Marquee screen saver, follow these steps:

1. Select Marquee and choose Setup. A dialog box similar to the one shown in Figure 3-15 appears. Pay attention to the Text Example box; it demonstrates the result of your customizations.

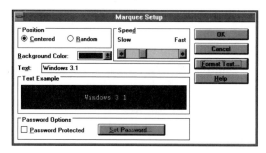

FIGURE 3-15. *The Marquee Setup dialog box.*

2. If you want the text to scroll across the middle of the screen, select Centered. For text to scroll at random heights from the bottom of the screen, select Random.

3. Select the speed at which the text scrolls.

4. Select the background color from the Background Color drop-down list box.

5. Type the text to be scrolled into the Text text box. If you'd like to format the text, choose Format Text. A dialog box similar to the one shown in Figure 3-16 appears. The Sample box demonstrates the results of the formatting.

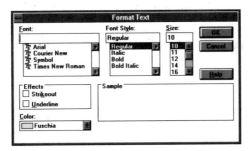

FIGURE 3-16. *The Format Text dialog box.*

6. Select the text's font from the Font list box.

7. Select the text's style from the Font Style list box.

8. Select the text's size from the Size list box.

9. Select any text effects you want in the Effects box.

10. Select the text's color in the Color drop-down list box.

11. Choose OK when the text is formatted correctly.

12. If you'd like to use password protection, see the section on passwords below.

13. Choose OK.

Setting Up Mystify

To set up the Mystify screen saver, follow these steps:

1. Select Mystify and choose Setup. A dialog box similar to the one shown in Figure 3-17 appears.

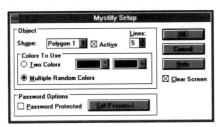

FIGURE 3-17. *The Mystify Setup dialog box.*

2. Select a polygon from the Shape drop-down list box. (To see the shapes, choose OK and choose Test in the Desktop dialog box, and then choose Setup to return to the Mystify Setup dialog box.)

3. Type the number of lines you want the shape to have into the Lines text box.

4. Select either Two Colors or Multiple Random Colors. If you select Two Colors, select the colors from the drop-down list boxes.

5. Select Clear Screen if you want Mystify to clear the screen before drawing its shapes.

6. If you'd like to use password protection, see the section on passwords below.

7. Choose OK.

Setting Up Starfield Simulation

To set up the Starfield Simulation screen saver, follow these steps:

1. Select Starfield Simulation and choose Setup. A dialog box similar to the one shown in Figure 3-18 appears.

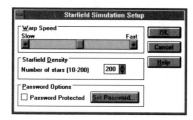

FIGURE 3-18. *The Starfield Simulation Setup dialog box.*

2. Select the speed at which the stars move.

3. Select the number of stars.

4. If you'd like to use password protection, see the section on passwords below.

5. Choose OK.

Setting Passwords

When password protection is enabled, you can't return to Windows from a screen saver without typing the password. To use password protection, follow these steps:

1. Select Password Protection.

2. Select Set Password. A dialog box similar to the one shown in Figure 3-19 appears.

FIGURE 3-19. *The Change Password dialog box.*

3. If you've previously set a password, type the old password into the Old Password text box. (This helps prevent someone from altering your password.)

4. Type the password you desire into the New Password text box.

5. Type the password again into the Retype New Password text box. (This is a safety check to make sure you typed the password correctly the first time.)

6. Choose OK.

Changing the Icon Spacing

Icon spacing is the distance (in pixels) Windows places between icons. To change the icon spacing, follow these steps:

 Click on the up or down arrow in the Spacing box in the Desktop dialog box to increase or decrease the value for icon spacing.

 Select the Spacing text box in the Desktop dialog box, and type in a new value for icon spacing.

Select the Wrap Title check box to allow Windows to wrap long icon names.

Using the Sizing Grid Box

The Sizing Grid box in the Desktop dialog box contains two fields. The first, *Granularity,* is a box you do not need to alter. The second, *Border Width,* lets you set the size of the window borders (which, by default, are 3 pixels wide).

To change the window border width, follow these steps:

 Click on the up or down arrow in the Border Width text box to increase or decrease the border width.

Select the Border Width text box, and type in a value for the new border width.

Changing the Cursor Blink Rate

To increase or decrease the rate at which your cursor blinks, follow these steps:

 Click on the left or right arrow in the Cursor Blink Rate scroll bar in the Desktop dialog box to make the cursor blink rate a little slower or faster, or drag the scroll box to rapidly change the rate.

 1. Select the Cursor Blink Rate scroll bar in the Desktop dialog box.

2. Use the arrow keys to move the Cursor Blink Rate scroll box. Watch the scroll box to determine the desired rate.

SETTING THE KEYBOARD RESPONSE

Keyboard response is controlled by two factors: how long your computer waits after you press a key to repeat the character of that key, and how quickly a held-down key repeats its character. To change the keyboard response, expand the Keyboard icon from the Control Panel. A dialog box similar to the one shown in Figure 3-20 appears.

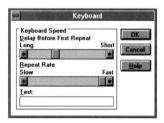

FIGURE 3-20. *The Keyboard dialog box.*

To change the delay before a pressed key repeats its character, follow these steps:

 Click on the left or right arrow in the Delay Before First Repeat scroll bar to increase or decrease the delay, or drag the scroll box left or right.

Use the Left or Right arrow key to increase or decrease the delay.

To change the key repeat rate, follow these steps:

 Click on the left or right arrow in the Repeat Rate scroll bar to make the key repeat rate a little slower or faster, or drag the scroll box to rapidly change the key repeat rate.

 1. Select the Repeat Rate scroll bar.

2. Use the Left or Right arrow key to adjust the key repeat rate.

To test the keyboard response, select the Test text box and hold down a key. When you're satisfied with the keyboard response, choose OK.

CONFIGURING A PRINTER

If you add or change a printer, you use the Printers option to inform Windows of the change. When you expand the Printers icon from the Control Panel, a dialog box similar to the one shown in Figure 3-21 appears.

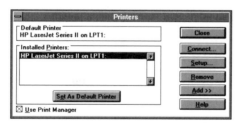

FIGURE 3-21. *The Printers dialog box.*

Adding a Printer

To add a printer, follow these steps:

1. Choose Add >>. The dialog box changes to look similar to the one shown in Figure 3-22.

2. Select the desired printer from the List of Printers list box.

3. Choose Install.

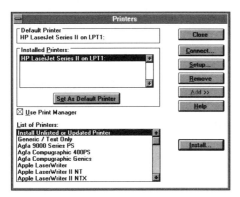

FIGURE 3-22. *The Printers dialog box, with a list of available printers.*

4. A dialog box similar to the one shown in Figure 3-23 appears. Insert the requested disk into the disk drive, and choose OK. (You can type a different drive letter and path into the text box, if necessary.)

FIGURE 3-23. *The Install Driver dialog box.*

Connecting a Printer to a Port

Before you can print, you must identify the port to which your printer is attached. Follow these steps:

1. Select the printer to which you want to connect from the Installed Printers list box in the Printers dialog box.

2. Choose Connect. A dialog box similar to the one shown in Figure 3-24 appears.

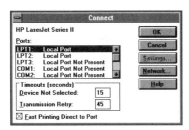

FIGURE 3-24. *The Connect dialog box.*

3. Select a port for the printer, and then choose OK.

   NOTE: *If you need to set specific printer options for the printer to which you're connecting, choose Setup in the Printers dialog box. A dialog box with options specific to the selected printer appears. Depending on your printer, you might be able to select a paper source, a paper size, and the number of copies to print. Some printers even let you scale high-resolution graphics and change the orientation of the page. See your printer's manual for the proper settings for these options.*

Connecting to a Network Printer

To connect to a network printer, follow these steps:

1. Choose the printer in the Installed Printers list box in the Printers dialog box.

2. Choose Connect. A dialog box similar to the one shown in Figure 3-24 appears.

3. Choose Network. A dialog box similar to the one shown in Figure 3-25 appears.

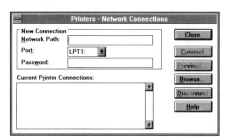

FIGURE 3-25. *The Printers-Network Connections dialog box.*

4. Type the network path to the printer into the Network Path text box. If you're unsure of the network path, see your network administrator.

   NOTE: *Some networks allow you to choose Browse to see a list of available network printers.*

5. Choose a port from the Port drop-down list box.

6. Type the printer's password into the Password text box, if necessary. If you're unsure of the printer's password, see your network administrator.

7. Choose Connect.

8. Choose Close in the Printers-Network Connections dialog box, and then choose OK in the Connect dialog box.

Removing a Printer

To remove a printer from the Installed Printers list, follow these steps:

1. Select the name of the printer to be removed from the Installed Printers list.

2. Choose Remove. A dialog box appears asking you to confirm the printer's removal. Choose Yes to remove the printer, or No to cancel the procedure.

Selecting the Default Printer

If your computer has multiple printers attached, you must select one printer as the default printer. Unless you specify otherwise, all print files are sent to the default printer. You can change the default printer at any time. To select a default printer, follow these steps:

1. Select a printer from the Installed Printers list.

2. Choose Set As Default Printer.

SPECIFYING INTERNATIONAL SETTINGS

To specify the date, time, number, and currency formats—as well as the keyboard layout—that Windows is to use, expand the Control Panel's International icon. A dialog box similar to the one shown in Figure 3-26 appears.

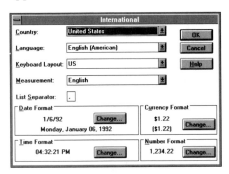

FIGURE 3-26. *The International dialog box.*

The following paragraphs describe the fields in this dialog box. To change the value of one of the first four fields, follow these steps:

1. Select the field, and open its drop-down list box.

2. Choose an item from the list.

Country This field controls the country whose date, time, number, and currency formats Windows uses. When you choose a country, Windows changes the formats in the Date, Time, Currency, and Number boxes (at the bottom of the International dialog box) to reflect the default formats used in that country.

Language This field controls the language that Windows-based applications use when sorting lists and converting the case of letters.

Keyboard Layout This field controls the keyboard layout Windows uses. The keyboard layout accommodates special characters for each country's language.

Measurement This field controls the measurement system Windows uses.

List Separator This field controls the symbol used to separate items in a list. To use a different symbol, select the List Separator box and type in the new symbol.

Date Format You can change the format used to display the date within applications that have a date function. For example, you can vary the order of month-day-year or change the punctuation used to separate the parts of the date. To change the date format, choose Change in the Date Format box. A dialog box similar to the one shown in Figure 3-27 appears.

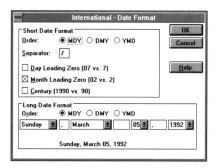

FIGURE 3-27. *The International-Date Format dialog box.*

The Short Date Format displays the date as three numbers representing the month, day, and year. You specify the order and number of digits for each part of the date. The Long Date Format displays the date as a combination of words and numbers. Select the options that suit your needs, and then choose OK.

Time Format You can choose either the 12-hour or 24-hour format, specifying the separator between the parts and displaying numbers representing the hours before 10 with a leading zero if you want. To change the time format, choose Change in the Time Format box. A dialog box similar to the one shown in Figure 3-28 appears. Select the options that suit your needs and choose OK.

FIGURE 3-28. *The International-Time Format dialog box.*

Currency Format To change the currency format, choose Change in the Currency Format box. A dialog box similar to the one shown in Figure 3-29 appears. Select the options that suit your needs and choose OK.

FIGURE 3-29. *The International-Currency Format dialog box.*

Number Format You can control the way numbers are displayed in Windows and in many Windows-based applications. To do so, choose Change in the Number Format box. A dialog box similar to the one shown in Figure 3-30 appears. Select the options that suit your needs and choose OK.

FIGURE 3-30. *The International-Number Format dialog box.*

SETTING THE COMPUTER'S DATE AND TIME

To change the computer's internal date and time, expand the Control Panel's Date/Time icon. A dialog box similar to the one shown in Figure 3-31 appears.

FIGURE 3-31. *The Date & Time dialog box.*

Setting the Computer's Date

To set your computer's date, follow these steps:

1. Click on the date field you want to change.
2. Click on the Date box's up or down arrow to increase or decrease the value in that field.

Select the date field you want to change, and type in the new value for that field.

Setting the Computer's Time

To set your computer's time, follow these steps:

1. Click on the time field you want to change.
2. Click on the Time box's up or down arrow to increase or decrease the value in that field.

Select the time field you want to change, and type in the new value for that field.

After you finish setting the date and time, choose OK.

SETTING NETWORK OPTIONS

If your computer is connected to a network, the Control Panel window includes a *Network* icon. If you expand this icon, a dialog box specific to your network appears, which might let you log onto the network, modify your user name and password, and send messages to other network users. See your network administrator for specific details.

USING MIDI MAPPER

MIDI stands for Musical Instrument Digital Interface. It allows several devices, instruments, and computers to send and receive messages to and from each other for the purpose of creating music, sound, or lighting.

You can use the Control Panel's MIDI Mapper option to select a MIDI setup for a sound device; create a new setup; or edit existing key maps, patch maps, and channel mappings. Windows supplies MIDI setups for the sound devices it supports. Unless you connect a synthesizer to the MIDI output port of your computer, you do not need to use the MIDI Mapper to create or edit a MIDI setup.

USING 386 ENHANCED MODE OPTIONS

If you own a computer that uses an 80386SX, 80386, i486SX, i486, or compatible microprocessor, Windows runs in 386 Enhanced mode. 386 Enhanced mode lets one or more applications not designed for Windows run at the same time as Windows-based applications.

When Windows-based applications and MS-DOS–based applications are running simultaneously, they sometimes try to use a device, such as a printer or modem, at the same time. (Such jockeying for resources is called *device contention.*) To specify how Windows is to handle this situation, follow these steps:

1. Expand the 386 Enhanced icon from the Control Panel. A dialog box similar to the one shown in Figure 3-32 appears.

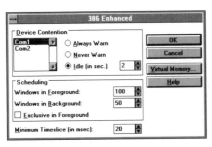

FIGURE 3-32. *The 386 Enhanced dialog box.*

2. Select the device from the Device Contention list.

3. Select the option button that best suits your needs. The following table describes the options:

Windows Action	Result
Always Warn	Windows displays a warning dialog box each time an application tries to use a device already in use. The dialog box asks you to choose the application to gain control of the device
Never Warn	Windows lets any application use the device at any time: You receive no warning. This might result in two applications trying to use the device at the same time, with undesirable results
Idle	Specifies the number of seconds (from 1 through 999) a device is to be idle before a second application can use it freely. If a second application tries to use the device before the idle period is complete, a warning message appears

386 Enhanced Mode Scheduling Options

When multiple applications are running simultaneously, Windows runs one application for awhile and then switches to the next application and runs it for a certain amount of time, repeating the process for each application. You can dictate how much time Windows spends on the application in the active window (called the *foreground* window) and how much time it spends on an application in an inactive window (called a *background* window). To do so, follow these steps:

1. Expand the 386 Enhanced icon from the Control Panel. A dialog box similar to the one shown in Figure 3-32 appears.

2. Select the Windows in Foreground text box, and enter a number from 1 through 10,000. Use this option to specify how much time Windows spends running a Windows-based application when it is in the foreground and an MS-DOS–based application is in the background.

3. Select the Windows in Background text box, and enter a number from 1 through 10,000. This number controls how much time Windows spends running a Windows-based application when it is in the background and an MS-DOS–based application is in the foreground.

4. Select Exclusive in Foreground to specify that Windows-based applications get 100 percent of the computer's processing time whenever a Windows-based application is active. (MS-DOS–based applications in the background are suspended.)

5. Select the Minimum Timeslice text box, and enter a number from 1 through 1000. This is the number of milliseconds (thousandths of a second) that Windows spends executing an application.

Understanding Windows Swap-Files

When Windows gets low on memory, it temporarily copies information to a file on your hard disk. When the information is needed again, Windows copies it back from the file into memory. This process of moving information from memory to a file on the hard disk and back to memory again is called *swapping*. The file to which information is copied is called a *swap-file.*

Windows supports two types of swap-files: *temporary* and *permanent*. A permanent swap-file is often a better choice because Windows can access a permanent swap-file more quickly. A permanent swap-file does, however, take up hard-disk space—even when Windows is not in use. If you use Windows extensively in 386 Enhanced mode, the permanent swap-file provides the best performance. If you don't use Windows extensively, you might want to sacrifice performance for available hard-disk space and use a temporary swap-file instead.

To create a swap-file, follow these steps:

1. Choose Virtual Memory in the 386 Enhanced dialog box. A dialog box similar to the one shown in Figure 3-33 appears.

FIGURE 3-33. *The Virtual Memory dialog box.*

2. If you're satisfied with your existing swap-file, choose Cancel; otherwise, choose Change. The Virtual Memory dialog box changes to resemble Figure 3-34.

3. Choose the drive on which the swap-file is to reside from the Drives drop-down list box.

4. Choose the swap-file's type from the Type drop-down list box.

5. Type in the size of the swap-file in the New Size text box.

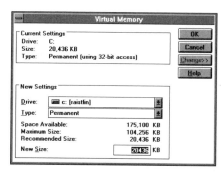

FIGURE 3-34. *The expanded Virtual Memory dialog box.*

6. Choose OK. Windows asks you whether you want to make changes to your virtual memory settings. Choose Yes to make the changes.

7. Windows tells you that you need to restart Windows so that the changes you made can take effect. Choose Restart Windows to immediately restart Windows, or choose Continue to continue the current session (the changes you made take effect the next time you start Windows).

MANAGING DEVICE DRIVERS

Device drivers allow hardware devices such as sound cards and video players to communicate with Windows. A new Windows 3.1 Control Panel option—Drivers—lets you install, remove, and configure device drivers. When you expand the Drivers icon, a dialog box similar to the one shown in Figure 3-35 appears.

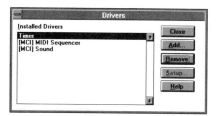

FIGURE 3-35. *The Drivers dialog box.*

Adding a Device Driver

To add a device driver, follow these steps:

1. Select Add. The Add dialog box, similar to the one shown in Figure 3-36, appears.

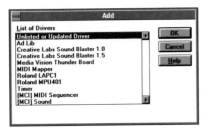

FIGURE 3-36. *The Add dialog box.*

2. Select the desired driver from the List of Drivers list box and choose
   OK. (If the desired device driver is not listed, select Unlisted or Updated Driver.) The Install Driver dialog box, similar to the one shown
   in Figure 3-37, appears. Insert the requested disk into the disk drive
   and choose OK. (You can type a different drive and path into the text
   box if necessary.)

FIGURE 3-37. *The Install Driver dialog box.*

3. After Windows installs the device driver, it displays a dialog box
   similar to the one shown in Figure 3-38. Select the port and interrupt
   that the device uses, and then choose OK.

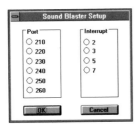

FIGURE 3-38. *The Sound Blaster Setup dialog box.*

4. Windows needs to restart before the device driver can take effect.
   Windows displays a dialog box similar to the one shown in Figure
   3-39, asking whether you want to restart Windows now. Remove the
   disk from the disk drive and choose Restart Now.

FIGURE 3-39. *The System Setting Change dialog box.*

Removing a Device Driver

If Windows has a device driver installed that you don't use, removing the device driver frees up memory for other uses. To remove a device driver, follow these steps:

1. Select the device driver you want to remove in the Installed Drivers list box in the Drivers dialog box. Choose Remove.

2. Windows displays a dialog box similar to the one shown in Figure 3-40, asking you to confirm the deletion. Choose Yes.

FIGURE 3-40. *The Remove dialog box.*

3. Windows needs to restart before the device driver can be removed. Windows displays a dialog box similar to the one shown in Figure 3-41. Choose Restart Now.

FIGURE 3-41. *The System Setting Change dialog box.*

Reconfiguring a Device Driver

As you add hardware to your computer, you might find that one device driver conflicts with another. To solve this problem, configure one of the device drivers to use a different port or interrupt. To configure a device driver, follow these steps:

1. Select the device driver to be configured in the Installed Drivers list box in the Drivers dialog box. Choose OK.

2. Windows displays a dialog box similar to the one shown in Figure 3-38. Select the port and interrupt that the device uses, and then choose OK.

ASSIGNING SOUNDS TO DIFFERENT SYSTEM EVENTS

By default, Windows beeps when you try to do something you are not allowed to do. (For example, you hear a beep when you try to move the cursor past the end of a Write document.) The Control Panel Sound option lets you turn the warning beep on and off. In addition, if you have installed a sound board and a sound device driver, you can assign various sounds to different system events. When you expand the Sound icon, a dialog box similar to the one shown in Figure 3-42 appears. (If you haven't installed a sound card, items in the Events and Files list boxes appear dimmed and are not selectable.)

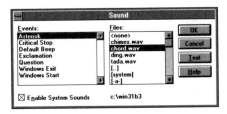

FIGURE 3-42. *The Sound dialog box.*

To enable system sounds, select the Enable System Sounds check box. To disable system sounds, deselect the check box.

To assign a sound to a specific system event, follow these steps:

1. Select the event to which you want to assign the sound from the Events list box.

2. Select the sound you want to assign from the Files list box. To hear the sound, choose Test. This assigns the sound to the event.

To remove a sound from an event, follow these steps:

1. Select the event from which you want to remove the sound from the Files list box.

2. Select the <none> option from the Files list box. This option restores the normal PC beep.

3. Choose OK.

PART IV

Desktop Applications

Windows provides a powerful collection of *desktop applications,* which are productivity tools designed to help you perform a variety of tasks directly from the Windows desktop:

Calculator	Performs business and statistical calculations
Calendar	Manages your appointments
Cardfile	Lists information
Clock	Keeps track of the time
Notepad	Allows you to edit ASCII text files
Paintbrush	Allows you to create figures and drawings
Recorder	Records macros
Terminal	Permits telecommunications
Write	Allows you to perform word processing
Character Map	Lets you insert special characters and symbols into documents
Object Packager	Allows you to place an icon that represents an embedded or linked object into a file
Media Player	Allows you to control multimedia hardware such as a sound card or a CD-ROM drive
Sound Recorder	Lets you play, record, and edit sound files

These programs are found in the Accessories group window, shown in Figure 4-1.

FIGURE 4-1. *The Accessories group window.*

This section provides an overview of each desktop accessory program. First, however, are two sets of actions available to most Windows desktop applications: Page Setup options and Printer options.

PAGE SETUP OPTIONS

Several Windows accessories—including Paintbrush, Notepad, and Cardfile—allow you to set the margins and add formatted headers and footers to your printouts.

Setting Margins

To set the margins of your printouts, follow these steps:

1. Choose Page Setup from the application's File menu. The Page Setup dialog box, similar to the one shown in Figure 4-2, appears.

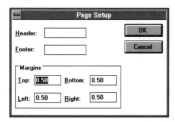

FIGURE 4-2. *The Page Setup dialog box.*

2. In the Margins area, type in the measurements you want for your margins.

3. Choose OK.

Inserting Headers and Footers

To insert a header or a footer into your printouts, follow these steps:

1. Choose Page Setup from the application's File menu. The Page Setup dialog box, similar to the one shown in Figure 4-2, appears.

2. Type the header or footer text into the Header or Footer text box. The table below includes the character codes used to format the header or footer.

Character Code	Function
&d	Inserts the current date
&p	Inserts the current page number

(continued)

continued

Character Code	Function
&f	Inserts the current filename
&l	Justifies the text following the code at the left margin
&r	Justifies the text following the code at the right margin
&c	Centers the text following the code
&t	Inserts the current time

3. Choose OK.

CHANGING PRINTERS AND PRINTER OPTIONS

Many Windows accessories allow you to set up a printer before print-ing. This includes selecting a printer (useful if you've installed several printers) and changing a printer's options. To change printers or printer options, follow these steps:

1. Choose Print Setup from the File menu. A dialog box similar to the one shown in Figure 4-3 appears.

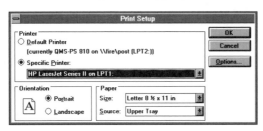

FIGURE 4-3. *The Print Setup dialog box.*

2. Select a printer from the Specific Printer drop-down list box, if necessary.

3. Select the Orientation and Paper specifications as necessary.

4. To set options specific to your printer, choose Options. A dialog box containing printer setup options appears.

5. Select printer options as necessary. The options in this dialog box vary depending on the printer you've installed. See your printer's manual for information about your printer's options, or press F1 for help.

6. Choose OK in the Print Setup dialog box.

CALCULATOR

The Calculator application acts as a *standard calculator* (for addition, subtraction, multiplication, and division) or as a *scientific calculator* (for trigonometric functions and statistical operations). The first time you use Calculator, the standard calculator, as shown in Figure 4-4, appears.

FIGURE 4-4. *The standard calculator.*

Switching Calculators

To switch between the standard and scientific calculators, choose either Standard or Scientific from the View menu.

Entering Values

To enter values, click on the number buttons or enter numbers with your keyboard.

NOTE: *If you're using the keyboard, you can use the numbers from the top row of the keyboard or the numbers from the numeric keypad. If you choose to use the numbers from the keypad, remember to first activate the NumLock key.*

Using the Standard Calculator

To add, subtract, multiply, or divide two numbers, follow these steps:

1. Enter the first number's digits.
2. Click on the symbol of the desired operation, or press the corresponding keyboard key.
3. Enter the second number's digits.
4. Click on the equal sign, or press your keyboard's equal-sign key.

The following table lists calculator buttons, the keyboard equivalent of each button, and the function of each button:

Button	Keyboard Key	Function
C	Esc	Clears the current calculation
CE	Delete	Clears the current value
Back	Backspace/ Left arrow	Clears the rightmost digit of the current value
MC	Ctrl+L	Clears the contents of memory
MR	Ctrl+R	Recalls the value stored in memory
M+	Ctrl+P	Adds the current value to the value in memory and places the result in memory
MS	Ctrl+M	Stores the current value in memory
+/−	F9	Changes the current value's sign
1/x	R	Calculates the reciprocal of the current value
sqrt	@	Calculates the square root of the current value
%	%	Treats the current value as a percentage
+	+	Adds
−	−	Subtracts
*	*	Multiplies
/	/	Divides
=	=	Performs the designated operation on the previous two values; choose again to repeat the operation
.	.	Inserts a decimal point into the current value

Using the Scientific Calculator

To use the scientific calculator, expand the Calculator icon in the Accessories group window and choose Scientific from the View menu. The scientific calculator appears as shown in Figure 4-5.

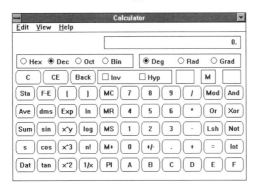

FIGURE 4-5. *The scientific calculator.*

Performing Scientific Calculations

With the scientific calculator you can work with hexadecimal, decimal, octal, or binary numbers and specify an angle's units of measure in degrees, radians, or gradients.

The following table lists the button, keyboard equivalent, and purpose of each scientific calculator function (the scientific calculator includes buttons found in the standard calculator):

Button	Keyboard Key	Function
(	(	Starts a new level of parentheses. The current level of parentheses is shown below the display. The maximum number of levels is 25
)	)	Closes the current level of parentheses
ABCDEF	ABCDEF	Enters the hexadecimal digits A through F. These keys can be used only in the hexadecimal number system
And	&	Calculates the bitwise exclusive AND of the current value
Ave	Ctrl+A	Calculates the average of the values in the Statistics Box. Inv+Ave calculates the average of the squares of the values in the Statistics Box
Bin	F8	Converts to the binary number system
Byte	F4	Displays the lower 8 bits of the current value
cos	o	Calculates the cosine of the current value. Inv+cos calculates the arc cosine of the current value. Hyp+cos calculates the hyperbolic cosine of the current value. Inv+Hyp+cos calculates the arc hyperbolic cosine of the current value
Dat	Ins	Enters the current number in the Statistics Box
Dec	F6	Converts to the decimal number system
Deg	F2	Sets trigonometric input for degrees when in decimal mode
dms	m	Converts the current value to degree-minute-second format. Inv+dms converts the current value to degrees
DWord	F2	Displays the full 32-bit representation of the current value
Exp	x	Allows entry of exponential numbers. Exp can be used only in the decimal number system

(continued)

continued

Button	Keyboard Key	Function
F-E	v	Turns scientific notation on or off. F-E can be used only with the decimal number system
Grad	F4	Sets trigonometric input for gradients when in decimal mode
Hex	F5	Converts to the hexadecimal number system
Hyp	H	Sets the hyperbolic function for sin, cos, and tan. These functions automatically turn off the hyperbolic function after a calculation is completed
Int	;	Displays the integer portion of the current value. Inv+Int displays the fractional portion of the current value
Inv	i	Sets the inverse function for sin, cos, tan, PI, x^y, x^2, x^3, ln, log, Ave, Sum, and s. These functions automatically turn off the inverse function after a calculation is completed
ln	n	Calculates the natural (base e) logarithm of the current value. Inv+ln calculates e raised to the power of the current value
log	l	Calculates the base 10 logarithm of the current value. Inv+log calculates 10 raised to the power of the current value
Lsh	<	Bitwise shifts the current value left. Inv+Lsh bitwise shifts the current value right
Mod	%	Displays the modulus (remainder) of $x \div y$
n!	!	Calculates the factorial of the current value
Not	~	Calculates the bitwise inverse of the current value
PI	p	Displays the value of π. Inv+PI displays $2 \times \pi$
Rad	F3	Sets trigonometric input for radians when in decimal mode
Oct	F7	Converts to the octal number system
Or	¦	Calculates the bitwise OR of the current value
s	Ctrl+D	Calculates standard deviation with the population parameter as $n1$. Inv+s calculates standard deviation with the population parameter as n
sin	s	Calculates the sine of the current value. Inv+sin calculates the arc sine of the current value. Hyp+sin calculates the hyperbolic sine of the current value. Inv+Hyp+sin calculates the arc hyperbolic sine of the current value

(continued)

continued

Button	Keyboard Key	Function
Sta	Ctrl+S	Activates the Statistics Box and its associated buttons
Sum	Ctrl+T	Calculates the sum of the values in the Statistics Box. Inv+Sum calculates the sum of the squares of the values in the Statistics Box
tan	t	Calculates the tangent of the current value. Inv+tan calculates the arc tangent of the current value. Hyp+tan calculates the hyperbolic tangent of the current value. Inv+Hyp+tan calculates the arc hyperbolic tangent of the current value
Word	F3	Displays the lower 16 bits of the current value
x^2	@	Squares the current value. Inv+x^2 calculates the square root of the current value
x^3	#	Cubes the current value. Inv+x^3 calculates the cube root of the current value
x^y	y	Computes x to the yth power. Inv+x^y calculates the yth root of x
Xor	^	Calculates the bitwise exclusive OR of the current value

Performing Statistical Calculations

To perform statistical calculations, expand the Calculator icon in the Accessories group window and choose Scientific from the View menu. Choose the scientific calculator's Sta button. Calculator opens a window called the *Statistics Box* which, like any window, can be moved to a convenient location on your screen. The Statistics Box appears as shown in Figure 4-6.

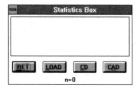

FIGURE 4-6. *The Statistics Box.*

To enter numbers into the Statistics Box, follow these steps:

1. Activate the Calculator window by clicking on it or by typing *R*.

2. Enter the desired value.

3. Click on Dat or press Ins.

You can enter as many values as you want. After entering all values, you can use the Calculator's statistical functions. If you enter more than six values into the Statistics Box, a vertical scroll bar appears at the right side of the list box. You can use this scroll bar to scroll through the values. The following table describes each Statistics Box button, as well as its keyboard equivalent, and purpose:

Button	Keyboard Key	Function
Ret	R	Returns to the Calculator window from the Statistics Box
Load	L	Copies the value selected in the Statistics Box to Calculator
CD	C	Deletes the value selected in the Statistics Box
CAD	A	Deletes all values from the Statistics Box

CALENDAR

Calendar is an electronic daily and monthly planner. Using Calendar, you can enter and track your appointments for today, next week, or even several months from now. Depending on your preference, Calendar lets you combine or separate your schedules. In other words, you can keep one large master schedule of all your appointments, or you can create individual schedules for home, work, and leisure activities. If your computer connects to a local area network, you can even exchange calendar files with other users to resolve scheduling conflicts. Using Calendar's built-in alarm capabilities, you can remind yourself of key appointments. Calendar lets you work with a daily or monthly planner, as shown in Figures 4-7 and 4-8.

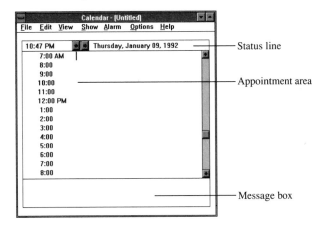

FIGURE 4-7. *The daily planner.*

FIGURE 4-8. *The monthly planner.*

Calendar File Operations

Calendar stores your schedules on disk in files with the CAL extension. Calendar's File menu lets you save a new schedule, save the existing schedule, print a list of appointments, or open a different calendar file, such as VACATION.CAL. The following table briefly describes Calendar's File menu:

Command	Function
New	Creates a new calendar, first prompting you to save or discard changes to the current calendar
Open	Displays a dialog box that lets you load an existing calendar file
Save	Saves schedule changes to an existing calendar file
Save As	Lets you save a schedule under a new name
Print	Prints appointments for the range of days you specify
Page Setup	Lets you define margins as well as insert a header and footer for each page
Print Setup	Lets you select a printer and change its options
Exit	Closes the Calendar window

The first time you start Calendar, the daily planner appears.

To select the planner you want to use, simply choose Day or Month from the View menu, or press F8 (daily planner) or F9 (monthly planner).

Calendar's Daily Planner

Calendar's daily planner lets you enter appointments for a 24-hour day.

Using the Daily Planner

To move inside the daily planner, use the arrow keys, or drag the vertical scroll bar using your mouse, and then click on the appropriate time. To schedule an appointment, simply type the appointment at the correct time. You can type notes to yourself in the message box at the bottom of the daily planner. Press Tab to move back and forth between the appointment area and the message box.

Changing Calendar's Timing

By default, Calendar divides a day into 1-hour intervals. If you need finer scheduling resolution, Calendar also lets you choose 15-minute and 30-minute intervals.

To change the daily appointment calendar's time interval, choose Day Settings from the Options menu. A dialog box similar to the one shown in Figure 4-9 appears.

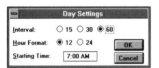

FIGURE 4-9. *The Day Settings dialog box.*

Interval lets you select 15-minute, 30-minute, or 60-minute intervals. *Hour Format* lets you specify a 12-hour clock with A.M./P.M. format or a 24-hour military clock. *Starting Time* lets you specify the hour of the day you want to appear at the top of the daily calendar when you first view it. Select the options you want, and then choose OK.

Viewing Other Appointments

Calendar lets you view a previous or future day's appointments. To do so, click on the scroll arrows in the status line, or press Ctrl+PgUp to view the previous day or Ctrl+PgDn to view the following day. To view the schedule for a day more than a few days prior to—or following—the current day, choose Date from Calendar's Show menu. A dialog box asks for the date. Type in the date of the schedule you want to view, and then choose OK.

Calendar's Edit Menu

Calendar lets you move or copy text using its Edit menu and the Windows Clipboard. The following table briefly describes Calendar's Edit menu:

Command	Function
Cut	Removes the selected text from Calendar and places it onto the Clipboard
Copy	Copies the selected text from Calendar onto the Clipboard
Paste	Copies text from the Clipboard to Calendar
Remove	Removes all Calendar appointments between a specified range of dates

The Edit menu Cut and Copy commands require that you first select the text to be cut or copied. To select text, follow these steps:

 Drag the mouse pointer over the desired text.

 Use the arrow keys to move the cursor to the beginning of the desired text. Hold down the Shift key and use the right and left arrow keys to select the desired text.

To remove a range of appointments, choose Remove from the Edit menu. A dialog box similar to the one shown in Figure 4-10 appears.

FIGURE 4-10. *The Remove dialog box.*

Type the range's beginning date into the From text box, the ending date into the To text box, and then choose OK. To remove the appointments for one day only, type the day's date into the From text box, leave the To text box empty, and choose OK.

Setting Alarms for Appointments

In the daily planner you can set alarms that notify you of appointments. To set an alarm, follow these steps:

1. Select the day for which you want the alarm set.

2. Click on the desired time, or move the cursor to the desired time by using the arrow keys.

3. Set the alarm by choosing Set from Calendar's Alarm menu.

A bell symbol—indicating that the alarm is set—appears to the left of the time.

Early warning By default, Calendar activates the alarm at the time you set for it. To sound the alarm a few minutes prior to the specified time, choose Controls from the Alarm menu. A dialog box similar to the one shown in Figure 4-11 appears.

FIGURE 4-11. *The Alarm Controls dialog box.*

Early Ring lets you specify the number of minutes prior to the specified time that you want the alarm to ring. *Sound* is a check box that lets you enable or disable the audible alarm.

NOTE: *For the alarm to be audible, Calendar must be running as either a window or an icon.*

Alarm styles At the scheduled time, Calendar beeps or plays the appropriate sound (if sound is enabled) and then notifies you of the alarm in one of the following ways:

- If Calendar is the active window, Calendar displays a reminder dialog box.

- If Calendar is a nonactive window, Calendar's title bar blinks. Activate Calendar's window to display the reminder dialog box.

- If Calendar is an icon, the icon blinks. Expand the icon to display the reminder dialog box.

NOTE: *If you are running an application designed for MS-DOS when the alarm sounds, Calendar might not be able to notify you of the alarm until the application completes.*

Calendar's Monthly Planner

From a monthly calendar you can select a specific day and view the day's appointments by double-clicking on the day or by highlighting the day with the arrow keys and pressing Enter.

To move to a previous or future month, click on the scroll arrows that appear in the status line, or press Ctrl+PgUp (previous month) or Ctrl+PgDn (following month).

Keyboard Combinations

The following table briefly summarizes Calendar's keyboard
combinations:

Keyboard Combination	Function
Ctrl+X or Shift+Delete	Cuts selected text onto the Clipboard
Ctrl+C or Ctrl+Ins	Copies selected text onto the Clipboard
Ctrl+V or Shift+Ins	Pastes text from the Clipboard into the daily planner
F8	Selects the daily planner
F9	Selects the monthly planner
F4	Moves to a specific day's appointments
Ctrl+PgUp	Selects the previous day or month
Ctrl+PgDn	Selects the following day or month
F5	Sets or removes an alarm
F6	Marks a special day on the monthly planner
F7	Inserts a unique time (not necessarily an interval of 15, 30, or 60 minutes) on the daily planner
F1	Opens Calendar's online help

NOTE: *Calendar obtains the current date and time from your computer's internal clock. If the date and time are incorrect, use the Date/Time option in the Control Panel to reset them.*

CARDFILE

Cardfile lets you organize information on electronic ''index cards.''
These cards can store a list of names and addresses, birthdays, phone
numbers, or virtually any other type of information.

Starting Cardfile

Expand the Cardfile icon from the Accessories group window. A window similar to the one shown in Figure 4-12 appears.

Creating a New Set of Cards

If you are creating a new set of cards, start Cardfile (choose New from
the File menu if Cardfile is already running) and type text in the card's
information area.

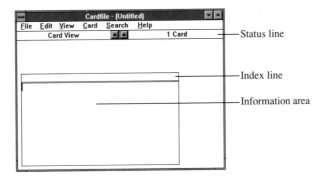

FIGURE 4-12. *A new Cardfile window.*

Assigning an Index

The card's top line is the *index line*. To assign an index to a card, follow these steps:

1. Double-click on the card's index line, or select Index from the Edit menu. The Index dialog box appears.

2. Type in a meaningful and—ideally—unique index that describes the card, and then choose OK.

Adding a Card

To add a card, follow these steps:

1. Choose Add from the Card menu. The Add dialog box appears.

2. Type in a meaningful and—ideally—unique index that describes the card's eventual contents, and then choose OK.

3. When Cardfile displays the card, type in the card's contents in the information area.

Saving a Cardfile

To save your cards, follow these steps:

1. Choose Save As from the File menu. The Save As dialog box appears.

2. Type in the filename you want. If you specify the name of an existing file, Cardfile displays a dialog box asking whether you want to replace the existing file. Note that if you choose Yes, you lose the information in the existing file.

Loading a Cardfile

To load previously created cards into a Cardfile, follow these steps:

1. Choose Open from the File menu. The Open dialog box appears.

2. Select the drive on which the cards are stored from the Drives drop-down list box.

3. Select the directory in which the cards are stored from the Directories list box.

4. Type the filename into the File Name text box, or select a file from the list box.

5. Choose OK.

The File Menu

The following table briefly describes Cardfile's File menu:

Command	Function
New	Starts a new list of cards, asking whether you want to save changes to the current card list, if any
Open	Displays a dialog box that lets you load an existing card file
Save	Saves the list of cards to an existing file
Save As	Lets you save a list of cards with a new name
Print	Prints the current card
Print All	Prints every card in the list
Merge	Combines the current list of cards with another card list
Page Setup	Lets you define margins as well as insert a header and a footer for each page
Print Setup	Lets you select a printer and change its options
Exit	Exits Cardfile

Looking Through Your Cards

Cardfile gives you several ways to look through your cards.

Moving Forward and Backward

To move forward or backward through the list, click on the scroll arrows in the status line, or use one of the key combinations listed in the following table:

Key Combination	Movement
PgUp	Moves backward one card
PgDn	Moves forward one card
Ctrl+Home	Moves to the first card in the list
Ctrl+End	Moves to the last card in the list
Ctrl+*X*	Moves to the first card whose index line begins with *X*. If two or more cards' index lines begin with the same letter or number, press Ctrl+*X* again to move to the second card, and so on

Moving with the View Menu

Choose List from the View menu to display the cards as a list of scroll-able index lines. Cardfile always lists cards alphabetically by index line.

Moving with the Search Menu

Cardfile's Search menu provides two ways to search for a card: You can search by index line or by keyword.

Searching by index line To search a set of cards for a specific index line, follow these steps:

1. Choose Go To from the Search menu. The Go To dialog box appears.

2. Type in the desired index line, and choose OK.

If Cardfile locates a matching index line, the matching card appears at the top of the deck. A dialog box informs you if no match is found.

Searching by keyword To search through the text of the cards for a matching word or phrase, follow these steps:

1. Choose Card from the View menu.

2. Choose Find from the Search menu. A dialog box similar to the one shown in Figure 4-13 appears.

FIGURE 4-13. *The Find dialog box.*

3. Type the text you want to search for into the Find What text box.

4. Select Match Case if you want Cardfile to distinguish between upper-case and lowercase letters.

5. Select a direction for the search.

6. Choose Find Next.

7. When your search is complete, choose Cancel in the Find dialog box.

If Cardfile locates a card with matching text, the card containing the match appears at the top of the deck. If—despite the match—this is not the card you want, you can continue the search by choosing Find Next again. A dialog box informs you if no match is found.

Editing Cards

To change a card's contents, follow these steps:

1. Choose Card from the File menu.

2. Move to the desired card.

3. Use the arrow, Delete, and Backspace keys to delete and insert text as necessary.

Undoing an Editing Change

To undo an editing change, choose Undo from the Edit menu. To undo all editing changes to the top card, choose Restore from the Edit menu.

Changing a Card's Index Line

To change a card's index line, follow these steps:

1. Move to the desired card.

2. Choose Index from the Edit menu. A dialog box appears asking for a new index line.

3. Type in the new index line and choose OK.

Selecting Text

To select text, follow these steps:

Position the mouse pointer over the start of the text, hold down the left mouse button, and then drag the mouse pointer to the end of the text. Release the left mouse button.

Move the cursor to the beginning of the text, hold down the Shift key, and then use the arrow keys to move the cursor to the end of the text. Release the Shift key.

Deleting a Card

To delete a card, follow these steps:

1. Move to the desired card.

2. Choose Delete from the Card menu.

3. A dialog box appears asking you to confirm the deletion. Choose OK to delete the card, or Cancel to terminate the procedure.

Copying Text from One Card to Another

To copy text from one card to another, follow these steps:

1. Select the desired text.

2. Choose Copy from the Edit menu.

3. Move to the card to which you want to copy the text. Move the cursor to the location where you want the text.

4. Choose Paste from the Edit menu.

Pasting a Paintbrush Graphic into a Card

To paste a graphic created by Paintbrush into a card, follow these steps:

1. Switch to Paintbrush.

2. Open an existing graphic that you want to paste into a card, or create a new graphic.

3. Use the Pick or the Scissors tool to select the graphic.

4. Choose Copy from the Edit menu.

5. Switch to Cardfile.

6. Choose Picture from the Edit menu.

7. Choose Paste from the Edit menu.

Linking a Paintbrush Graphic to a Card

When you link a graphic to a card, a copy of the graphic is displayed in the card but the graphic is still stored in its original Paintbrush file. When you make changes to the graphic, these changes appear in every file that contains a link to that graphic.

To link a graphic from Paintbrush, follow these steps:

1. Switch to Paintbrush.

2. Open an existing graphic that you want to link, or create a new graphic.

3. Save your new graphic or any changes you've made to the existing graphic.

4. Use the Pick or the Scissors tool to select the graphic.

5. Choose Copy from the Edit menu. A copy of the graphic is placed onto the Clipboard.

6. Switch to Cardfile.

7. Open the file containing the card to which you want to link the graphic.

8. Choose Picture from the Edit menu.

9. Choose Paste Link from the Edit menu. Or you can choose the Paste Special command to specify the format of the graphic. If you want to change the format to a bitmap or a picture, choose the Paste Special command. If you want the graphic to remain in the Paintbrush Picture format, there is no need for you to choose the Paste Special command.

CLOCK

The most straightforward application is Clock. Clock displays the current time and date, using either an analog clock or a digital clock, as shown in Figure 4-14.

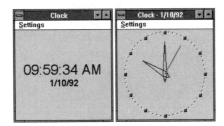

FIGURE 4-14. *The Clock window.*

The first time you start Clock a digital clock appears. To select the analog clock, choose Analog from the Settings menu. To change back to a digital clock, choose Digital from the Settings menu. When you change the clock type, the new type remains in effect—even if you leave Windows—until you specifically change it again.

Setting Clock's Font

The digital clock lets you change the font used to display the date and time. To change Clock's font, follow these steps:

1. Choose Set Font from the Settings menu. A dialog box appears, similar to the one shown in Figure 4-15.

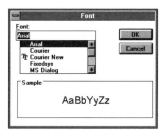

FIGURE 4-15. *The Font dialog box.*

2. Select the desired font from the Font list box. The Sample box displays several characters drawn in the selected font.

3. Choose OK.

Hiding or Displaying Clock's Title Bar

To hide Clock's title bar, choose No Title from the Settings menu. A faster method of hiding Clock's title bar is to double-click on Clock's window, or press Esc. To display Clock's title bar, click on Clock's window or press Esc. A fast method of displaying Clock's title bar with the mouse is to double-click on Clock's window.

Hiding or Displaying the Date

If you choose an anolog clock, Clock displays the current date in its title bar. If you choose a digital clock, Clock displays the current date beneath the time. To hide the date, choose Date from the Settings menu. To display the date again, choose Date from the Settings menu.

Hiding or Displaying Seconds

By default, Clock displays seconds in the current time. To hide the seconds, choose Seconds from the Settings menu. To display seconds again, choose Seconds from the Settings menu.

Setting Clock to Be the Topmost Window

Normally, the window of the active application is the topmost window. Clock is special, however—it can be set to remain the topmost window regardless of the active application. To set clock to be the topmost window, follow these steps:

1. Minimize Clock's window.

2. Select Always on Top from Clock's Control menu.

3. Restore Clock's window, if desired.

Restoring Clock

To restore clock, follow these steps:

1. Minimize Clock's window.

2. Select Always on Top from Clock's Control menu.

3. Restore Clock's window, if desired.

You can select the clock and then minimize Clock's window to an icon, displaying the current time at the bottom of the screen. This arrangement gives you constant access to the clock but leaves you free to work with other Windows-based applications.

NOTE: *Clock obtains the current time from your computer's internal clock. If the time is incorrect, use the Date/Time option in the Control Panel to reset it.*

NOTEPAD

Notepad is a simple text editor that lets you create memos, record notes, or create batch files.

NOTE: *The maximum size of a Notepad document is about 50,000 characters.*

Starting Notepad

To start Notepad, expand the Notepad icon from the Accessories group window. A window similar to the one shown in Figure 4-16 appears.

Opening a Document

If you want to load an existing document, follow these steps:

1. Choose Open from the File menu. The Open dialog box appears.

2. Type in the name of the document you want to open, or select it (and its directory, if necessary) from the Files and Directories list boxes. Then choose OK.

FIGURE 4-16. *A new Notepad window.*

Creating a New Document

To create a new document, choose New from the File menu. (If you've made changes to the current document, a dialog box appears, asking whether you want to save the changes.)

Saving a Document

To save a document, choose Save from the File menu. If this is the first time you've saved the file, the Save As dialog box appears. Simply type in the desired filename. (If a file with that name already exists, a dialog box asks whether you want to replace the existing file. If you choose Yes, the information in the existing file is lost.)

NOTE: *Notepad does not create a backup file for documents. When you save a changed document, the previous document is lost.*

Notepad's File Menu

The following table briefly describes the commands available in the File menu:

Command	Function
New	Creates a new document, first prompting you to save or discard any changes to the current document
Open	Displays a dialog box that lets you load an existing document
Save	Saves the current document
Save As	Saves the current document with a new name
Print	Prints the document
Page Setup	Lets you define margins as well as insert a header and a footer for each page
Print Setup	Lets you select a printer and change its options
Exit	Closes the Notepad window

Advanced File Editing

The following table describes the commands available in Notepad's Edit menu.

Command	Function
Undo	Cancels the most recent edit
Cut	Deletes the selected text and places it onto the Clipboard
Copy	Copies the selected text from the file onto the Clipboard
Paste	Copies the contents of the Clipboard to the current document at the cursor's location
Delete	Removes the selected text from the document without placing the text onto the Clipboard
Select All	Selects all of the document's text
Time/Date	Inserts the time and date at the cursor location
Word Wrap	Enables word wrapping at the right edge of the window

Notepad Notes

- By default, Notepad does not wrap text, so you must press Enter at the end of each line. (To have Notepad perform word wrapping, choose Word Wrap from the Edit menu.)

- To move through a document, use the arrow, PgUp, PgDn, Home, and End keys, or the vertical and horizontal scroll bars if you're using a mouse.

The following table lists keyboard combinations that help you move around the screen:

Keyboard Combination	Function
Home	Moves the cursor to the start of the current line
End	Moves the cursor to the end of the current line
Ctrl+Home	Moves the cursor to the start of the document
Ctrl+End	Moves the cursor to the end of the document
PgUp	Moves the cursor up one page
PgDn	Moves the cursor down one page
Ctrl+Right Arrow	Moves the cursor right one word
Ctrl+Left Arrow	Moves the cursor left one word

Moving Text

To move text to a different location in the document, follow these steps:

1. Select the desired text, and choose Cut from the Edit menu. The text disappears from your screen.

2. Move the cursor to where you want the text to reappear, and choose Paste from the Edit menu. The text reappears at the cursor location.

Searching for a Word or a Phrase

To search a document for a word or a phrase, follow these steps.

1. Choose Find from the Search menu. A dialog box appears, similar to the one shown in Figure 4-17.

FIGURE 4-17. *The Find dialog box.*

2. Type in the text you want to find.

3. Select the Match Case check box if Notepad must match uppercase and lowercase letters exactly.

4. Select the direction you want Notepad to search (down toward the end of the document; or up toward the beginning of the document).

If the search is successful, the desired portion of text appears in the Notepad window. A dialog box informs you if no match occurs. If a match occurs but is *not* the match you want, choose Find Next again. Choose Cancel to close the Find dialog box.

Controlling Notepad's Printed Output

If you choose Page Setup from Notepad's File menu, a dialog box appears, similar to the one shown in Figure 4-18. This dialog box lets you specify a *header* (a line of text that appears at the top of each page) and a *footer* (a line of text that appears at the bottom of each page). This dialog box also lets you specify the page's margin sizes (in inches).

To use the Page Setup dialog box, simply fill in the fields as desired, and then choose OK. By default, the header contains the filename and the footer contains the page number.

FIGURE 4-18. *The Page Setup dialog box.*

Place the following special characters in either the header or footer text to enhance your printed output:

Character Code	Function
&l	Justifies the text following the code at the left margin
&r	Justifies the text following the code at the right margin
&c	Centers the text following the code
&d	Inserts the current date
&f	Inserts the current filename
&p	Inserts the current page number
&t	Inserts the current time

Creating a Time-Log Document

If the first line of your document contains the characters *.LOG* (capital letters required), Notepad creates a *time-log document*. Each time you open a time-log document, Notepad appends the current time and date to the document. If you start your new text after the time and date appears, you will have a log of your work. Using the Search menu, you can quickly find a specific day's work.

PAINTBRUSH

Paintbrush lets you create your own graphics images or enhance graphics images created by a scanner.

NOTE: *If you try to use Paintbrush without a mouse, you'll quickly become frustrated. Accordingly, this section focuses on mouse operations. For more information on keyboard combinations—and for a detailed description of the Paintbrush program—see* Windows 3.1 Companion *(Microsoft Press, 1992).*

Starting Paintbrush

To start Paintbrush, expand the Paintbrush icon from the Accessories group window. A window appears, similar to the one shown in Figure 4-19.

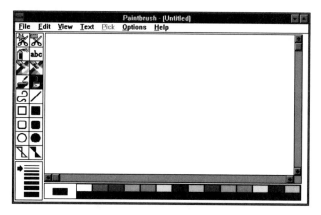

FIGURE 4-19. *A new Paintbrush window.*

Using the File Menu

The following table describes the commands available in Paintbrush's File menu:

Command	Function
New	Creates a new image, first prompting you to save or discard any changes to the current image
Open	Displays a dialog box that lets you load an existing image
Save	Saves the current image
Save As	Displays a dialog box that lets you save the current image with a new name
Page Setup	Lets you define printer margins as well as insert a header and a footer for each page
Print	Prints the current image
Printer Setup	Lets you select a printer and change its options
Exit	Closes the Paintbrush window

Paintbrush provides a collection of drawing tools described here:

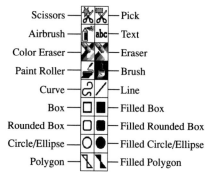

Tool	Function
Scissors	Selects a free-form portion of the image to move or delete
Pick	Selects a rectangular portion of the image to move or delete
Airbrush	Spray-paints the image with the foreground color
Text	Places text into the image
Color Eraser	Changes portions of the foreground color to the background color, or changes every occurrence of one color to another
Eraser	Changes portions of the drawing to the background color
Paint Roller	Fills an area with the foreground color
Brush	Paints using the foreground color
Curve	Draws a smooth curved line
Line	Draws a straight line
Box	Draws an unfilled rectangle
Filled Box	Draws a rectangle filled with the foreground color
Rounded Box	Draws an unfilled rectangle with rounded corners
Filled Rounded Box	Draws a rectangle with rounded edges, filled with the foreground color
Circle/Ellipse	Draws an unfilled ellipse
Filled Circle/Ellipse	Draws an ellipse filled with the foreground color
Polygon	Draws an unfilled irregular shape
Filled Polygon	Draws an irregular shape filled with the foreground color

Selecting a Tool

To select a tool, simply click on the tool.

Selecting Line Thickness

Below the Paintbrush tool set are eight horizontal lines of varying thickness. You use these lines to define the thickness Paintbrush uses to draw or erase lines and shapes. To change the thickness, simply click on the desired thickness.

Selecting Colors

To the right of the line-size box is the color palette, along with the foreground and background color indicator. To select a foreground color, simply click (using the left mouse button) on the desired color. To select a background color, click (using the right mouse button) on the desired color.

NOTE: *If you have swapped the functions of the mouse buttons, as described in Part III, you'll use the right button to select the foreground color and the left button to select the background color.*

Using the Paintbrush Tools

The following sections briefly describe the use of each Paintbrush tool.

Working with the Scissors Tool

The Scissors tool lets you select an irregularly shaped area. (After creating this "cutout," you can perform a variety of operations on it. See "Fun with Cutouts" later in this section.)

To use the Scissors tool, follow these steps:

1. Select the Scissors tool. The mouse pointer changes to a pair of cross hairs.

2. Place the mouse pointer on the starting point of the area to select.

3. Hold down the mouse button, and then draw around the area you want to select. After you completely encircle the area, release the mouse button.

Working with the Pick Tool

The Pick tool provides a convenient way to cut out a rectangular area. (After creating such a "cutout," you can perform a variety of operations on it. See "Fun with Cutouts" later in this section.)

Working with Your Image

The following tips should prove helpful as you begin to create and work with Paintbrush images:

■ If your image is larger than the canvas area, use the horizontal and vertical scroll bars to view different parts of the image.

■ Choose Zoom In from the View menu to temporarily magnify a portion of the image to allow detailed editing. (While you're zoomed in, you edit pixel-by-pixel with each click of the mouse.) After you finish with the detailed editing, choose Zoom Out from the View menu to restore the image to its normal size.

To use the Pick tool, follow these steps:

1. Select the Pick tool. The mouse pointer changes to a pair of cross hairs.

2. Place the mouse pointer at the upper left corner of the rectangular area you want to select.

3. Hold down the mouse button, and then move the mouse pointer to create a rectangular border around the desired area. Then release the mouse button.

Copying a Paintbrush Image onto the Clipboard

To copy a Paintbrush image onto the Clipboard, use either the Pick or the Scissors tool to select the image, and then choose Copy from the Edit menu. The image can then be pasted from the Clipboard into another application.

Working with the Airbrush

The Airbrush tool works like a can of spray paint, letting you shade areas. By selecting different line sizes and colors, you can change the Airbrush tool's effect.

Fun with Cutouts

Cutouts can be treated in a variety of different ways. The following table provides a simple description of the operations available. Experiment! Or, for further information, see *Windows 3.1 Companion* (Microsoft Press, 1992).

Operation	Description
Cut	Removes the cutout from the window and places it onto the Clipboard
Copy	Places a copy of the cutout onto the Clipboard
Paste	Pastes a copy of the Clipboard into the window
Flip Horizontal	Flips the cutout from side to side
Flip Vertical	Flips the cutout from top to bottom
Inverse	Inverts the cutout colors to their complementary colors
Shrink + Grow	Allows you to copy and size a cutout
Tilt	Allows you to copy and skew a cutout
Clear	Changes the background area within the original cutout to the background color when you choose Shrink + Grow or Tilt

To use the Airbrush tool, follow these steps:

1. Select the Airbrush tool. The mouse pointer changes to a pair of cross hairs.

2. Select a foreground color.

3. Press the mouse button to airbrush an area. Hold down the mouse button, and drag the mouse to airbrush a large area. Release the mouse button to shut the Airbrush off. By concentrating the Airbrush in an area, you can create darker shades.

Adding Text to an Image

Many images you create will need labels, titles, or other text. The Text tool lets you add text to an image. Depending on your image, you will want to select an appropriate font, font size, and text attribute such as bold, italic, or underline. The commands in the Text menu let you do just that.

To add text to your image, follow these steps.

1. Select the Text tool. The mouse pointer changes to an I-beam.

2. Select as the foreground color the color you'd like the text to be.

3. Select Fonts from the Text menu. A dialog box similar to the one shown in Figure 4-20 appears.

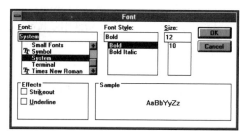

FIGURE 4-20. *The Font dialog box.*

4. Select a font from the Font list box.

5. Select a font style from the Font Style list box.

6. Select a font size from the Size list box.

7. Click on OK to close the Font dialog box.

8. Click on the location where you'd like the text to appear. Type in the desired text.

Erasing Areas

Paintbrush's Color Eraser tool and Eraser tool let you erase areas of the image. The Color Eraser, however, only erases text or graphics of the selected foreground color, replacing it with the background color. The selected line size affects how much area the erasers remove at one time. A thick line erases more area, whereas a thin line gives you finer control.

To erase an area, follow these steps:

1. Select either the Color Eraser tool or the Eraser tool. The mouse pointer changes to a pair of cross hairs inside a square.

2. Select the foreground and background colors.

3. Move the mouse pointer to the area you want to erase.

4. Hold down the mouse button, and then drag the mouse to erase the area.

5. After you finish erasing, release the mouse button.

Changing All of One Color to Another

To quickly change all of one color to another, follow these steps:

1. Select as the foreground color the color you wish to change.

2. Select as the new color the background color.

3. Double-click on the Color Eraser tool.

Using the Paint Roller Tool

The Paint Roller tool lets you fill a bordered area with the foreground color. If the border has an opening, the color leaks through the border, filling outer areas.

To use the Paint Roller, follow these steps:

1. Select the Paint Roller tool. The mouse pointer changes to look like a paint roller.

2. Select as the foreground color the desired color.

3. Move the mouse pointer into the area you'd like to fill, and press the mouse button.

Using the Brush Tool

The Brush tool lets you draw using the foreground color and line thickness. To use the Brush tool, follow these steps:

1. Select the Brush tool. The mouse pointer changes to a square.

2. Select as the foreground color the desired color.

3. Select the desired line thickness. The size of the mouse pointer changes to reflect your choice.

4. Move the mouse pointer to the desired location. Hold down the mouse button, and move the mouse to draw.

5. After you finish drawing, release the mouse button.

Drawing Lines

The Curve tool and the Line tool let you draw curved and straight lines. To create a straight line, follow these steps:

1. Select the Line tool. The mouse pointer changes to a pair of cross hairs.

2. Select as the foreground color the desired color.

3. Select the desired line thickness.

4. Click where you want the line to begin, and drag the mouse to create the desired shape. Then release the mouse button.

To draw a curved line, follow these steps:

1. Select the Curve tool. The mouse pointer changes to a pair of cross hairs.

2. Select as the foreground color the desired color.

3. Select the desired line thickness.

4. Click where you want the line to begin, and drag the mouse to create the desired shape. Then release the mouse button.

5. Next hold down the mouse button and drag. The line curves to follow the mouse pointer. When the line has the desired shape, release the mouse button. If you're satisfied with the shape, click on the second endpoint to finalize the curve. If you want to add a second curve to the line, click and drag again.

Drawing Boxes

Paintbrush lets you draw four types of boxes: empty boxes, empty boxes with rounded corners, filled boxes, and filled boxes with rounded corners. (The border of a filled box is drawn with the background color, and then filled with the foreground color.)

To draw a box, follow these steps:

1. Select the desired box tool. The cursor changes to a pair of cross hairs.

2. Select the desired foreground color. For a filled rectangle, also select a background color.

3. Select the desired line thickness.

4. Move the mouse pointer to the location where you want the box to appear. Drag the mouse to create the desired shape, and then release the mouse button. To draw a perfect square, press the Shift key before releasing the mouse button.

Creating Circles and Ellipses

Paintbrush lets you create empty or filled circles and ellipses. An *ellipse* is simply an elongated circle. (The border of a filled circle or ellipse is drawn with the background color and then filled with the foreground color.)

To draw a circle or an ellipse, follow these steps:

1. Select the desired circle/ellipse tool. The cursor changes to a pair of cross hairs.

2. Select the desired foreground color. For a filled circle or ellipse, also select a background color.

3. Select the desired line thickness.

4. Move the mouse pointer to the location where you want the circle or ellipse to appear. Drag the mouse to create the desired shape, and then release the mouse button. (You'll have the tendency to create an ellipse. If you want to ensure that you draw a true circle, press the Shift key before you release the mouse button.)

Creating Polygons

A *polygon* is an irregularly shaped closed object. Paintbrush lets you create empty and filled polygons. To create a polygon, follow these steps:

1. Select a polygon tool. The mouse pointer changes to a pair of cross hairs.

2. Select the desired foreground color. For a filled polygon, also select a background color.

3. Select the desired line thickness.

4. Move the mouse pointer to the location of the first corner of the border of the polygon you want to draw and click.

5. Move the mouse pointer to the location of the second corner of the border of the polygon you want to draw and click. A line appears between the first and second corners.

6. Move the mouse pointer to the location of the next corner of the border of the polygon you want to draw and click. A line appears

between the second and third corners. Repeat this process for each corner of the polygon. Finish the polygon by clicking on the starting point.

RECORDER

As you work with Windows on a regular basis, you might find yourself repeatedly opening the same windows and running the same applications. To save time and keystrokes, you can create a Windows *macro*. A Windows macro is a record of the keystrokes and mouse operations required to perform a certain task. The Recorder application lets you record to a macro the keystrokes and mouse operations you perform on a regular basis. When you later need to perform the operation, you can run the macro to perform the steps automatically.

Starting Recorder

To start Recorder, expand the Recorder icon from the Accessories group window. A window similar to the one shown in Figure 4-21 appears.

FIGURE 4-21. *A new Recorder window.*

Recording a Macro

Normally, you use the mouse to select and choose options. However, this can cause problems in a macro because options such as menus, check boxes, and option buttons aren't always in the same place. To avoid this problem, it's wise to use keyboard combinations rather than the mouse when selecting and choosing options to be recorded as a Windows macro.

To record a Windows macro, follow these steps:

1. Choose Record from the Macro menu. A dialog box similar to the one shown in Figure 4-22 appears.

2. Type a descriptive macro name in the Record Macro Name text box, but do *not* press Enter.

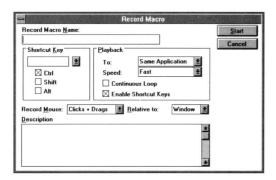

FIGURE 4-22. *The Record Macro dialog box.*

3. Move to the Shortcut Key text box, and select a shortcut key combination you want to use to run the macro. For example, if you want the keyboard combination Ctrl+Alt+T to run this macro, type T in the Shortcut Key text box, and then select the Ctrl and Alt check boxes. (Do not select a keyboard combination used by the application your macro assists.) If you want to use a special key (such as F1) in the shortcut key combination, select the key from the Shortcut Key drop-down list box.

4. The default selections for the remaining options are probably fine. You might want to include a description of the macro in the Description box.

5. Start the application in which the macro is to be used, and then return to the Record Macro dialog box.

6. Choose Start to begin recording. The Recorder window becomes a blinking icon on the desktop to indicate that the recording process has begun.

7. Perform the operations you want to record.

8. After you finish performing the operations you want to record, expand the Recorder icon. A dialog box similar to the one shown in Figure 4-23 appears.

FIGURE 4-23. *The Recorder dialog box.*

9. Select Save Macro, and choose OK.

Saving a Macro File

To save a macro file on disk, follow these steps:

1. Choose Save As from the File menu. The Save As dialog box appears.

2. Select a drive and directory from the Drives drop-down list box and the Directories list box, type a filename into the File Name text box, and choose OK. If a file with that name already exists, Recorder displays a second dialog box asking whether you want to replace the existing file. Choose Yes to replace it or No to cancel the operation.

Loading a Macro File

To load a macro file, follow these steps:

1. Choose Open from the File menu. The Open dialog box appears, asking for the name of the macro file.

2. Select a drive and directory from the Drives drop-down list box and the Directories list box, type the filename into the File Name text box, and choose OK. Recorder shows the names of each macro in the file.

Running a Macro

To run a macro, both Recorder and the macro's application must be running, and the macro file must be loaded. To run a macro, press the macro's shortcut key.

Deleting a Macro

To delete a macro, follow these steps:

1. In the Recorder window, select the macro to be deleted.

2. Choose Delete from the Macro menu. A dialog box appears, asking you to confirm the deletion. Choose Yes.

Other Recorder Options

Select or deselect the following commands from the Options menu to control how Recorder operates:

Command	Function
Control+Break Checking	When enabled, allows Ctrl+Break or Ctrl+C to stop a Windows macro
Shortcut Keys	When enabled, allows use of Windows keyboard combinations with macros
Minimize On Use	When enabled, reduces the Recorder to an icon when a Windows macro is run
Preferences	Lets you change several default macro settings

TERMINAL

Terminal is a telecommunications application that lets one computer exchange information with another, typically via telephone lines.

Starting Terminal

To start Terminal, expand the Terminal icon from the Accessories group window. The Terminal window appears, similar to Figure 4-24.

FIGURE 4-24. *A new Terminal window.*

Identifying Your Modem

Terminal needs to know what type of modem you are using. To provide this information, follow these steps:

1. Choose Modem Commands from the Settings menu. A dialog box similar to the one shown in Figure 4-25 appears.

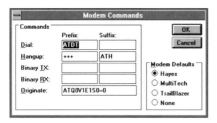

FIGURE 4-25. *The Modem Commands dialog box.*

2. If your modem is listed in the Modem Defaults box, select the option button that corresponds to it. If your modem is not listed, select the Hayes option button.

3. Select the Prefix field of the Dial text box. The letters *ATDT* tell the modem your phone uses touch-tone dialing. If your phone is rotary based, change these letters to *ATDP*. The remaining options in this dialog box are fairly standard, and you probably do not have to change them unless explicitly directed by your modem documentation.

4. Choose OK.

Setting Up Communication Parameters

Before two computers can communicate, they must agree on a set of communication parameters, such as baud rate and the number of bits. If you access several different computers, each might use a unique set of data communication parameters. To set these up appropriately, follow these steps:

1. Choose Communications from the Settings menu. A dialog box appears, similar to the one shown in Figure 4-26.

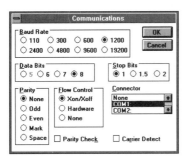

FIGURE 4-26. *The Communications dialog box.*

2. Select a port from the Connector list box and the data communication settings used by the computer you'll be calling. (You'll need to find this out from the owner of the other computer.)

Setting Up a Phone Number

Specify the phone number of the computer you want to call. To do so, follow these steps:

1. Choose Phone Number from the Settings menu. A dialog box appears, similar to the one shown in Figure 4-27.

FIGURE 4-27. *The Phone Number dialog box.*

2. Type in the number of the computer you intend to call. Type it in as you would dial it. (That is, if you must dial 9 to access an outside line, include the 9 in the Dial text box. If the phone call is long distance, include a 1 and the area code.) You can separate digits with spaces, parentheses, or hyphens. A comma directs the modem to

pause two seconds before continuing dialing. (This is useful to give an office phone system time to connect with an outside line.)

The remaining fields let you tell Terminal what steps to perform if a modem at the other end of the phone line fails to respond in the specified time period:

☐ Timeout If Not Connected In lets you specify how long the computer tries to make a connection. Depending on how far you are calling and on the number of times the phone rings before the other modem answers, you might need to increase the timeout period to 60 seconds or more.

☐ Redial After Timing Out lets you direct Terminal to keep recalling until it connects to the other computer.

☐ Signal When Connected directs Terminal to beep to notify you of the connection when it successfully connects to the other computer.

3. After you finish setting options, choose OK.

Saving Communication Information

To save the communication information, choose Save As from the File menu. A dialog box appears asking you for a filename. Type in a filename, and choose OK. (Unless you specify otherwise, Terminal saves the file with a TRM filename extension.)

Loading Communication Information

To load the communication information back into Terminal, choose Open from the File menu. A dialog box appears, asking what file to load. Type in the filename, and choose OK.

Placing a Phone Call

After you assign the data communication parameters and phone number, you're ready to place a call. To do so, follow these steps:

1. Choose Dial from the Phone menu. A dialog box appears that displays the phone number being called, as well as a countdown of seconds until time-out. If Terminal successfully reaches the other modem, you might hear the two modems exchange tones as they form a connection.

2. When the tones end, press Enter to begin your interaction with the other computer.

3. When you're ready to end the connection, choose Hangup from the Phone menu. Terminal directs your modem to disconnect the call and hangs up the line.

Transferring Files

One of the primary reasons for connecting your computer to another computer is to exchange files. In general, the files you exchange are either text (ASCII files created by a text editor such as Notepad) or binary files such as programs, spreadsheets, or word processing files. Terminal lets you send and receive both kinds of files.

Sending Files

To send a file to another computer, follow these steps. (The other computer must be prepared to receive a file.)

1. To send a text file, choose Send Text File from the Transfers menu. To send a binary file, choose Send Binary File from the Transfers menu.

2. A dialog box appears. Type in the name of the file you want to send, and choose OK.

A small status bar that lets you monitor the transfer appears at the bottom of the window:

- If Terminal successfully transfers the file, the status bar disappears, and interactive mode resumes.

- If an error occurs during transmission, a dialog box appears describing the error. You might need to set a Text Transfer or Binary Transfer setting. For more information on these settings, use Terminal's online help, or refer to *Windows 3.1 Companion* (Microsoft Press, 1992).

Receiving Files

To receive a file, follow these steps:

1. To receive a binary file, choose Receive Binary File from the Transfers menu. To receive a text file, choose Receive Text File from the Transfers menu. A dialog box appears, prompting you for the name of the file to receive the text. (You can optionally append the text to an existing file.)

2. Type in the filename, and press Enter. If you're receiving a text file, the text from the remote computer scrolls by on the screen as Terminal captures it in the file. A status bar at the bottom of the window lets you monitor the number of bytes transferred.

3. To end the transmission, click on the Stop button, or choose Stop from Terminal's Transfer menu. If an error occurs, a dialog box describing the error appears.

WRITE

Write is a word-processing application that lets you create and edit professional-quality letters and reports. Beyond performing the normal editing tasks of cutting and pasting text, Write lets you align paragraphs, use different character fonts, and even integrate graphics images you create with Paintbrush.

Starting Write

To start Write, expand Write's icon from the Accessories group window. A window appears, similar to the one shown in Figure 4-28.

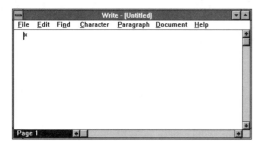

FIGURE 4-28. *A new Write window.*

Opening an Existing Document

To open an existing document, choose Open from Write's File menu. The Open dialog box appears. Select the drive and directory where the file is stored in the Drives drop-down list box and the Directories list box, and type the name of the file into the File Name text box. Then choose OK.

Creating a New Document

To create a new document, choose New from the File menu. If you've made any changes to the current document, Write first asks whether you want to save the changes to the current document.

Saving a Document

After you complete the document, you need to save it to a file on disk. To do so, choose Save As from Write's File menu. The Save As dialog box appears. Select the drive and directory on which the file is to be saved in the Drives drop-down list box and the Directories list box, and then type a filename into the File Name text box. Then choose OK.

Write's File Menu

The following table briefly describes the commands in Write's File menu.

Command	Function
New	Creates a new document, first asking whether you want to save any changes to the current document
Open	Lets you load an existing document
Save	Saves a document
Save As	Saves a document with a new name
Print	Prints the document
Print Setup	Lets you select a printer and change its options
Repaginate	Repaginates a document
Exit	Closes the Write window

Moving Through Your Document

You can move to a different area in your document by using either the mouse or the keyboard.

1. To move up or down one line at a time, click on the up or down arrow in the scroll bar.
2. To move up or down one screen at a time, click on the scroll bar above or below the scroll box.
3. To move rapidly to a new area, drag the scroll box up or down.

The table on the following page shows the key combinations you use to move to a different area of your document.

Keyboard Combination	Cursor Movement
Home	Moves the cursor to the start of the current line
End	Moves the cursor to the end of the current line
Ctrl+Home	Moves the cursor to the start of the document
Ctrl+End	Moves the cursor to the end of the document
PgUp	Moves the cursor up one page
PgDn	Moves the cursor down one page
Ctrl+PgUp	Moves the cursor to the top of the page
Ctrl+PgDn	Moves the cursor to the bottom of the page
Ctrl+Right arrow	Moves the cursor right one word
Ctrl+Left arrow	Moves the cursor left one word
Goto+Right arrow*	Moves the cursor to the next sentence
Goto+Left arrow*	Moves the cursor to the previous sentence
Goto+Down arrow*	Moves the cursor to the next paragraph
Goto+Up arrow*	Moves the cursor to the previous paragraph
Goto+PgDn*	Moves the cursor to the next page, according to the last repagination
Goto+PgUp*	Moves the cursor to the previous page, according to the last repagination

*Goto represents the numeric keypad 5 key.

Editing Your Document

Write lets you move, copy, or delete sections of your document. To use Write's edit menu, you must first select the text you want to manipulate. To do so, follow these steps:

Position the mouse pointer over the start of the text, hold down the mouse button, and then drag the mouse pointer to the last of the text you want to select. Then release the mouse button.

Move the cursor to the beginning of the text, hold down the Shift key, and then use the arrow keys to move the cursor to the end of the text you want to select. Then release the Shift key.

Moving Text

To move text from one location to another, follow these steps:

1. Select the text to move, and then choose Cut from the Edit menu.

2. Move the cursor to the location in the document where you want to place the text, and then choose Paste from the Edit menu.

Copying Text

To copy text from one location to another, follow these steps:

1. Select the text to copy, and then choose Copy from the Edit menu.

2. Move the cursor to the location in the document to which you want to copy the text. Choose Paste from the Edit menu. Repeat this step at each location to which you want to copy the text.

Deleting Text

To delete text, simply select the text, and choose Cut from the Edit menu.

Cutting and Pasting Graphics

Write lets you Paste graphics images into a document from the Clipboard. To place a graphics image you have created using Paintbrush (such as a logo) into your Write document, follow these steps:

1. Within Paintbrush, use the Scissors tool or the Pick tool to place the image onto the Clipboard. (See ''Paintbrush,'' earlier in this section.)

2. Start Write, and open the document in which the image is to be placed.

3. Move to the location in the document where you want the image to appear. Choose Paste from the Edit menu.

Sizing an image After you place the image into the document, you can resize it to suit your needs. To resize an image, follow these steps:

1. Select the image:

 Click on the image.

 Move the cursor to the beginning of the image, hold down the Shift key, and then press the Down arrow key.

2. Choose Size Picture from the Edit menu. A box appears around the image, and the mouse pointer changes to a box within a box shape.

3. Use the mouse or the arrow keys to resize the box surrounding the image. When the box is the correct size, click the mouse or press Enter. The image is redrawn at the new size.

Positioning an image After you place the image into the document, you can move it to suit your needs. To move an image, follow these steps:

1. Select the image:

 Click on the image.

 Move the cursor to the beginning of the image, hold down the Shift key, and then press the Down arrow key.

2. Choose Move Picture from the Edit menu. A box appears around the image, and the mouse pointer changes to a box within a box shape.

3. Use the mouse or the arrow keys to move the box surrounding the image. When the box is positioned properly, click the mouse or press Enter. The image is redrawn at the new location.

Using Embedded Objects

Write's Edit menu lets you place an embedded object or a link to an object within your document. For more information on links and embedded objects, refer to the section on Object Packager near the end of Part IV.

Using the Find Menu

The Find menu provides several ways of searching for text in a document.

Searching for a Word or a Phrase

To search your document for a string of text, follow these steps:

1. Choose Find from Write's Find menu. A dialog box appears, similar to the one shown in Figure 4-29.

FIGURE 4-29. *The Find dialog box.*

2. Type the text you are searching for into the Find What text box.

3. Select Match Whole Word Only if you want Write to distinguish the text from words containing the text (for example, if you want to find the word *book* and want to ignore the word *bookmark*).

4. Select Match Case if you want Write to match uppercase and lower-case letters exactly (for example, if you want to find *Book* but not *book*).

5. Choose Find Next. If Write finds the text in the document, it displays the part of the document containing the text; otherwise, Write displays a dialog box telling you the text was not found.

6. To search for another occurrence of the text, choose Find Next; otherwise, choose Cancel.

Changing a Word or a Phrase

Write lets you quickly search for and change each occurrence of a word or a phrase throughout your document. To change a word or a phrase, follow these steps:

1. Move to the location in the document where you want the changes to begin.

2. Choose Replace from the Find menu. A dialog box appears, similar to the one shown in Figure 4-30.

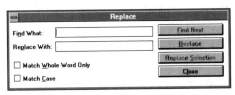

FIGURE 4-30. *The Replace dialog box.*

3. In the Find What text box, type the word or phrase you want to change, but do *not* press Enter. In the Replace With field, type the desired replacement word or phrase, but do *not* press Enter.

4. Select Match Whole Word Only if you want Write to distinguish the Find What text from words containing the text (for example, if you want to find the word *book* and want to ignore the word *bookmark*).

5. Select Match Case if you want Write to match uppercase and lower-case letters exactly (for example, if you want to find *Book* but not *book*).

6. Choose the "find" button that best suits your needs:

Find Button	Result
Find Next	Finds the next match but doesn't change it
Replace	Changes the current match

(continued)

continued

Find Button	Result
Replace All	Changes all matching text, starting from the beginning of the document
Replace Selection	Changes all occurrences of the Find What text in the selected portion of the document
Close	Cancels the replace operation

Moving to a Specific Page

To move to a specific page in the document, follow these steps:

1. Choose Go To Page from the Find menu. A dialog box appears, similar to the one shown in Figure 4-31.

FIGURE 4-31. *The Go To dialog box.*

2. Type in the number of the page to which you'd like to move, and then choose OK.

Changing Character Fonts

Write provides several character fonts for use in your Write documents. Write gives you two ways to select and use fonts: You can select a specific font, and then type. (The text you type appears in the new font.) Or you can change any existing text to a new font. To do so, follow these steps:

1. Select the desired text.

2. Choose Fonts from the Character menu. A dialog box appears, similar to the one shown in Figure 4-32.

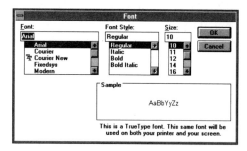

FIGURE 4-32. *The Font dialog box.*

3. Select a font from the Font list box, a font style from the Font Style list box, and a size from the Size list box, and then choose OK.

As you select different font, style, and size combinations, Write displays corresponding sample text.

Using the Character Menu

Write's Character menu lets you select text attributes such as bold, underline, or italic. Reduce Font and Enlarge Font incrementally decrease or increase a font size. For best results, use these commands with the TrueType fonts that come with Windows 3.1.

Using the Paragraph Menu

Write automatically wraps text at the right edge of the window. The only time you need to press Enter is to distinguish one paragraph in your document from another. Write's Paragraph menu lets you specify paragraph alignment, line spacing within paragraphs, and paragraph indentation. The following table briefly describes the formatting commands available from the Paragraph menu:

Commands	Function
Left	Aligns text along the left margin only
Centered	Centers text between the left and right margins
Right	Aligns text along the right margin only
Justified	Aligns text along the left and right margins
Single Space	Single-spaces a paragraph
1½ Space	Uses 1½ spaces between lines in a paragraph
Double Space	Double spaces a paragraph
Indents	Lets you set paragraph indents

NOTE: *If you have a mouse, you can set these paragraph values with the Ruler. See "Using the Document Ruler" later in this section.*

Changing Paragraph Alignment

To change a paragraph's alignment, follow these steps:

1. Place the cursor within the paragraph to align.

2. Select the desired alignment from the Paragraph menu.

Changing Paragraph Spacing

Write lets you single-space, double-space, or triple-space the lines of text in a paragraph. To change a paragraph's line spacing, perform the steps that follow.

1. Place the cursor within the desired paragraph.

2. Select the desired line spacing from the Paragraph menu.

Changing Paragraph Indentation

Write lets you indent a paragraph from the left and right margins. The first line can be indented separately to make it stand out. To indent a paragraph, follow these steps:

1. Place the cursor within the paragraph you want to change.

2. Choose Indents from the Paragraph menu. A dialog box appears, similar to the one shown in Figure 4-33.

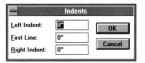

FIGURE 4-33. *The Indents dialog box.*

3. Type in the indentations you want, and then choose OK.

Using the Document Menu

Write's Document menu lets you control elements that affect your entire document.

Adding a Header or a Footer

A *header* is text—such as a title, your name, or a page number—that appears at the top of each page throughout your document. Likewise, a *footer* is text that appears at the bottom of each page. To add a header or a footer to your document, follow these steps:

1. Choose Header or Footer from Write's Document menu. A window appears where you type in the actual text for the header or footer, along with a dialog box that lets you provide certain information *about* the text, as shown in Figure 4-34.

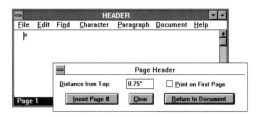

FIGURE 4-34. *The Header window and Page Header dialog box.*

2. Type the text for the header or footer into the Header window. When you're satisfied with the text, press Alt+F6 to move to the Header dialog box.

3. In the Distance from Top text box (if you're creating a footer, the text box is Distance from Bottom), specify a value—in inches—that dictates how far the header or footer falls from the top (header) or bottom (footer) of the page.

4. Select the Print on First Page check box if you want your header or footer to appear on the first page.

5. Choose Insert Page # if you want page numbers to accompany your header or footer.

6. If you're happy with your choices, choose Return to Document. If you'd like to revise your header or footer, press Alt+F6 to move to the Header window and edit your header or footer text. Or, if you want to start from scratch, simply choose Clear in the Page Header dialog box to erase the header or footer, and press Alt+F6. Begin again at step 2, above.

Setting Tab Stops

By default, Write sets tab stops at every half inch. You can set up to 12 tab stops of your own. To do so, follow these steps.

NOTE: *If you are using a mouse, you can set tabs with the document ruler. See "Using the Document Ruler" later in this section.*

1. Choose Tabs from Write's Document menu. A dialog box similar to the one shown in Figure 4-35 appears.

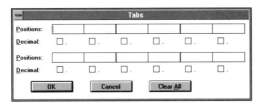

FIGURE 4-35. *The Tabs dialog box.*

2. Select an empty Positions text box.

3. Type in the tab stop's distance from the left margin in inches (include a " after the number).

4. Select the corresponding Decimal check box if you want to align decimal points in a column of numbers.

5. After you finish setting tab stops, choose OK.

Deleting a Tab Stop

To delete a tab stop, follow these steps:

1. Choose Tabs from the Document menu.

2. Select the Positions text box for the tab stop you want to remove.

3. Use the Backspace key to delete the measurement.

4. After you finish deleting tab stops, choose OK.

Using the Document Ruler

The *document ruler* is a ruler and a group of icons that Write displays below its menu bar to help you view and control tab stops, margins, and indentation, as shown in Figure 4-36.

Tab stop		Left align	
Decimal tab stop		Center	
Single space		Right align	
1½ space		Align left and right	
Double space			

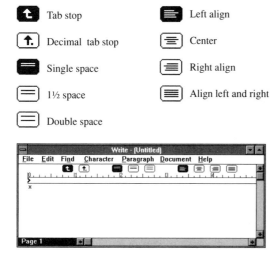

FIGURE 4-36. *The document ruler displays your screen measurements.*

To toggle the ruler on or off, choose Ruler On or Ruler Off from the Document menu.

Setting Tab Stops with the Document Ruler

To set tab stops with the document ruler, follow these steps:

1. Click on the icon for the type of tab stop you want (normal or decimal).

2. Click on the ruler at the location where you want the tab stop to appear.

Changing and Removing Tab Stops with the Document Ruler

To change a tab stop using the document ruler, drag the tab stop to its new location. To remove a tab stop, drag it below the document ruler.

Setting Paragraph Line Spacing with the Document Ruler

To set paragraph line spacing with the document ruler, follow these steps:

1. Click anywhere within the paragraph you want to format.

2. Click on the icon for the type of line spacing you want.

Setting Paragraph Alignment with the Document Ruler

To set paragraph alignment with the document ruler, follow these steps:

1. Click anywhere within the paragraph you want to format.

2. Click on the icon for the type of alignment you want.

Keyboard Combinations

The following table describes Write's keyboard combinations.

Keyboard Combination	Function
Ctrl+X _or_ Shift+Delete	Cuts selected text from the document and places it onto the Clipboard
Ctrl+C _or_ Ctrl+Ins	Copies selected text onto the Clipboard
Ctrl+V _or_ Shift+Ins	Pastes the contents of the Clipboard into the document at the cursor location
F3	Repeats the most recent Find operation
F4	Activates the Go To dialog box
Ctrl+B	Enables bold text
Ctrl+I	Enables italic text
Ctrl+U	Enables underlined text

CHARACTER MAP

Character Map is a Windows 3.1 desktop accessory that lets you insert onto the Clipboard characters and symbols from other character sets. You can then paste the characters and symbols from the Clipboard into documents. To start Character Map, expand the Character Map icon in the Accessories group window. A window appears, similar to the one shown in Figure 4-37.

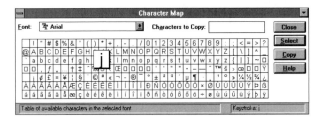

FIGURE 4-37. *The Character Map window.*

To insert characters and symbols onto the Clipboard using Character Map, follow these steps:

1. Select a font from the Font drop-down list box. The characters in Character Map's display change to those of the new font.

2. Select the desired character from Character Map's display. The selected character appears in an enlarged box, as shown in Figure 4-38.

FIGURE 4-38. *The selected character appears in an enlarged box.*

3. Choose Select. The character appears in the Characters to Copy text box.

4. Continue selecting as many characters as you want. After you select all the characters you desire, choose Copy.

5. Switch to the application into which the characters are to be inserted, and choose Paste from the Edit menu.

OBJECT PACKAGER

Object Packager is a tool you can use to insert a *package* into a document. A package is an icon that represents an embedded or a linked object. An embedded object is information created in one document and inserted into another document. An embedded object can be edited within that document even if a different application was used to create the object. A linked object is a representation of an object that is inserted into a document. The object exists in the original application and, when it is changed, the linked object updates to reflect these changes. An object may be a complete document or part of one. For example, a spreadsheet cell and an entire drawing are both objects.

When you expand the Object Packager icon, a window appears, similar to the one shown in Figure 4-39.

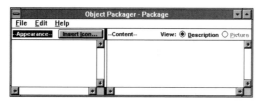

FIGURE 4-39. *The Object Packager window.*

The Object Packager window is split into two smaller windows. The window on the left, the Appearance window, displays the icon that represents the embedded or linked object in the destination document. The window on the right, the Content window, displays a desciption of the object by default. To see a graphical view of the object, select the Picture option button. To again see the description of the object, select the Description option button. Picture view is only available when the application that created the object is capable of creating linked and embedded objects.

Creating a Packaged Object

To create a packaged object, follow these steps:

1. From the File menu in Object Packager, choose Import. A dialog box appears, similar to the one shown in Figure 4-40.

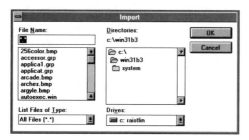

FIGURE 4-40. *The Import dialog box.*

2. In the Import dialog box, select the document you want to package and then choose OK. The icon of the application used to create the

file appears in the Appearance window, and the name of the file appears in the Content window.

3. Choose Copy Package from the Edit menu. A copy of the package is placed onto the Clipboard.

4. Switch to the application into which you want to place the package. The application must support embedded or linked objects.

5. If applicable, move the cursor to the place where you want the package to appear.

6. Choose Paste from the application's Edit menu.

Creating a Package That Contains Part of a Document

To create a package that contains part of a document, follow these steps:

1. Open the application containing the information you want to package. The application must be able to create objects that can be embedded in or linked to other applications.

2. Select the information you want to package.

3. Choose Copy from the application's Edit menu.

4. Open Object Packager.

5. Select the Content window.

6. Choose Paste from the Edit menu to embed the package, or choose Paste Link to link it.

7. Choose Copy Package from the Edit menu.

8. Switch to the application into which you want to insert the package. The application must support embedded or linked objects.

9. Move the cursor to the place you want the package to appear.

10. Choose Paste from the application's Edit menu. The package is embedded or linked and appears in the document. Open the package to see its contents.

NOTE: *You can embed or link documents by dragging their icons from File Manager into applications that support embedded or linked objects.*

Selecting a Different Icon

By default, Object Packager uses the icon of the application that created the information for an embedded or linked object. To use a different icon, follow these steps:

1. Choose Insert Icon in the Object Packager window. A dialog box appears, similar to the one shown in Figure 4-41.

FIGURE 4-41. *The Insert Icon dialog box.*

2. Select an icon from the Current Icon list box.

3. Choose OK. The Insert Icon dialog box closes, and the selected icon appears in the Appearance window.

Creating Your Own Icons

Object Packager also lets you use Paintbrush to create your own custom icons. To do so, follow these steps:

1. Start Paintbrush and create an image.

2. Use Paintbrush's Pick or Scissors tool to select the image.

3. Choose Cut from Paintbrush's Edit menu.

4. Start Object Packager.

5. Select Object Packager's Appearance window.

6. Choose Paste from Object Packager's Edit Menu. The image you created in Paintbrush appears in the Appearance window.

MEDIA PLAYER

Media Player is a multimedia desktop accessory program included with Windows 3.1. If your PC has the appropriate hardware, Media Player lets you play animation, sound, and MIDI sequencer files. To start Media Player, expand the Media Player icon in the Accessories group window. A window appears, similar to the one shown in Figure 4-42.

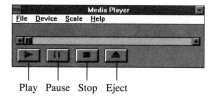

Play Pause Stop Eject

FIGURE 4-42. *The Media Player window.*

Selecting a Media Device

Media Player supports two device types: compound and simple. Compound devices are used to play a specific media file. When you select a compound device, a dialog box appears, prompting you for the name of the file you want to play. Simple devices, on the other hand, play the media loaded in the device itself. To select a device, follow these steps:

1. Choose the device from the Display menu. (Compound devices have ellipses [...] after their name.)

2. If you've chosen a compound device, the Open dialog box appears. Type in the name of the media file and choose OK.

NOTE: *The devices listed in the Device menu correspond to MCI (Multimedia Control Interface) devices you have installed in your system. For information on installing MCI devices, see Part III.*

Opening Media Files

If you are using a compound device, you can open and play other media files. To open a media file for a compound device, follow these steps:

1. Choose Open from the File menu. The Open dialog box appears.

2. Type in the name of the media file you want to open and choose OK.

Selecting a Scale

The Media Player Scale menu lets you display the scale in tracks or time intervals. To change the scale display, choose the option you want from the Scale menu.

Media Device's Buttons

Media Player is similar to a tape recorder, providing Play, Pause, Stop, and Eject buttons. Below is a table of Media Player's buttons, and the function each performs.

Button	Function
Play	Starts play
Pause	Pauses play
Stop	Stops play
Eject	Ejects a compact disk

Changing the Playback Position

The horizontal scroll bar in the Media Player window controls Media Player's playback position. To select a playback position, drag the scroll box to the location you want, or select the scroll box and use the left or right arrow keys to move it.

Exiting Media Player

To exit Media Player, choose Exit from the File menu.

SOUND RECORDER

Sound Recorder is a multimedia desktop accessory program included with Windows 3.1. If your PC has the appropriate hardware, Sound Recorder lets you play, edit, and record sound files in Wave format. To start Sound Recorder, expand the Sound Recorder icon in the Accessories group window. A window appears, similar to the one shown in Figure 4-43.

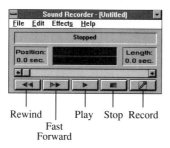

FIGURE 4-43. *The Sound Recorder window.*

Opening a Sound File

To open a sound file for playback or editing, follow these steps:

1. Choose Open from the File menu. The Open dialog box appears.

2. Type in the name of the sound file you want to open, and choose OK.

Sound Recorder's Buttons

Sound Recorder is similar to a tape recorder, providing Rewind, Fast Forward, Play, Stop, and Record buttons. A table of Sound Recorder's buttons and the function each performs is on the following page.

Button	Function
Rewind	Rewinds the sound file
Fast forward	Forwards the sound file
Play	Plays back the sound file
Stop	Stops playing the sound file
Record	Records a sound file

As you play back a sound file, the Sound Recorder displays the sound's waveform as if you were viewing the wave on an oscilloscope.

Recording a Sound File

The Sound Recorder lets you record up to 60 seconds of sound using a microphone attached to your computer. To record a new sound file, follow these steps:

1. Choose New from the File menu.

2. Choose Record.

3. Record up to one minute of sound.

4. Choose Stop.

5. Choose Save As from the File menu. The Save As dialog box appears. Type in a name for the file, and then choose OK.

Adding Sound to an Existing Sound File

To add sound to an existing sound file, follow these steps:

1. Choose Open from the File menu. The Open dialog box appears.

2. Type in the name of the sound file you want to open and choose OK.

3. Move the scroll box to the location at which you want to insert the new sound.

4. Choose Record.

5. Record the desired sound.

6 Choose Stop.

7. Play the new sound file. If you are satisfied, choose Save from the File menu; otherwise, go back to step 3.

Inserting a Sound File

To insert an existing sound file into your current sound file, follow these steps:

1. Move the scroll box to the location at which you want to insert the sound file.

2. Select Insert File from the Edit menu. The Insert File dialog box appears.

3. Type in the name of the sound file you want to insert, and choose OK.

3. Play your sound file. If you are satisfied, choose Save from the File menu; otherwise, discard the change and go back to step 1.

Mixing Sound Files

When you mix sound files, the Sound Recorder combines the sounds from two files so the sounds can be played back simultaneously. To mix two sound files, follow these steps:

1. Load the first sound file into Sound Recorder.

2. Move the scroll box to the location at which you want the mixing to begin.

3. Choose Mix from the File menu. The Mix With File dialog box appears.

4. Type in the name of the sound file you want to mix, and choose OK.

5. Play your new sound file. If you are satisfied, choose Save from the File menu; otherwise, go back to step 1.

Deleting Part of a Sound File

To delete part of a sound file, follow these steps:

1. Load the sound file you want into Sound Recorder.

2. Move the scroll box to the location you desire.

3. To delete all sounds in front of the location indicated by the scroll box, choose Delete Before Current Position from the Edit menu. To delete all sounds after the scroll box's location, choose Delete After Current Position from the Edit menu.

4. A dialog box asking you to confirm the deletion appears. Choose OK.

5. Play the sound file. If you are satisfied, choose Save from the File menu; otherwise, go back to step 1.

Discarding Changes to a Sound File

If you make changes to a sound file and are unhappy with the results, perform the steps that follow.

1. Select Revert from the File menu. A dialog box appears, asking you to verify the operation.

2. Select Yes. Sound Recorder restores the sound file to its last saved state.

Changing a Sound's Volume

To increase a sound's volume, choose Increase Volume (by 25%) from the Effects menu. To decrease a sound's volume, choose Decrease Volume from the Effects menu.

Changing the Speed at Which a Sound Is Played

To increase the speed at which a sound plays, choose Increase Speed (by 100%) from the Effects menu. To decrease the speed at which a sound plays, choose Decrease Speed from the Effects menu.

Adding an Echo to a Sound

To add an echo to a sound, choose Add Echo from the Effects menu.

Reversing a Sound

To reverse a sound, choose Reverse from the Effects menu. Choosing Reverse again restores the sound to its original direction.

Exiting Sound Recorder

To exit Sound Recorder choose Exit from the File menu.

PART V

Games

Windows 3.1 provides two computer games, Solitaire and Minesweeper. To select a game, open the Games group in the Program Manager window. The Games group window appears, similar to the one shown in Figure 5-1.

FIGURE 5-1. *The Games group window.*

PLAYING SOLITAIRE

To play Solitaire, expand the Solitaire icon in the Games group window. A new window appears, similar to the one shown in Figure 5-2.

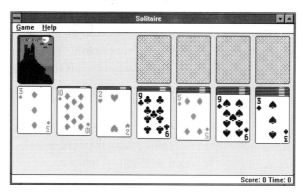

FIGURE 5-2. *The Solitaire window.*

The goal of Solitaire is to build, in the upper right-hand corner of the Solitaire window, four stacks of cards—one for each suit. The cards are stacked in order of rank, from Ace to King.

The seven lower columns of cards begin with one card in column 1, two cards in column 2, and so on up to seven cards in column 7. The top card of each column is placed face up, and the unexposed cards below it are placed face down.

Each card has a rank. Aces have the lowest rank and Kings have the highest rank. A card can be moved from one column to another, as long as the top card of the column you're moving to is ranked one card higher than the card you're placing and is a different color. For example, the Six of Hearts could be moved from one column to be placed on top of the Seven of Clubs in another column. Whenever a face-down card in one of these columns is exposed, the card can be turned face up.

In the same manner, a sequence of upturned cards can be moved to another column, as long as the top card of the other column has a higher rank and is a different color than the bottom card of the sequence.

Kings and Aces are special. Kings can be moved to vacated columns in the lower columns, whereas Aces can be moved to vacant stacks located in the upper right-hand corner of the Solitaire window. Top cards of the lower columns can be moved to these stacks, as long as the top card of the lower stack has a lower rank and is the same suit. For example, the Two of Hearts can be moved up onto the Ace of Hearts.

A deck of cards (stacked face down), in the upper left-hand corner of the Solitaire window, is turned over either one or three at a time, depending on the options you've chosen. The top card can be moved to either one of the lower columns or the upper stacks, as long as the rules of rank and color are satisfied. When all cards in this deck are turned over, the deck is turned face down (depending on what options you've chosen). Click on the empty box to begin turning over cards from this deck again.

Moving Cards

Moving a card is easiest with the mouse—simply drag the card to its new position. To move a card with the keyboard, follow these steps:

1. Move the pointer to the card using the left and right arrow keys.

2. Press either Enter or the Spacebar.

3. Move the pointer to the card's destination using the left and right arrow keys. The card moves with the pointer.

4. When the card is in position, press either Enter or the Spacebar.

Turning Cards Over

Turning cards over is easiest with the mouse—simply double-click on the card. To turn a card over with the keyboard, move the pointer to the card using the left and right arrow keys, and then press either Enter or the Spacebar.

Selecting a Card Design

Solitaire lets you choose the appearance of the back of your cards. To do so, follow these steps:

1. Choose Deck from the Game menu. A dialog box appears displaying sample card backs as shown in Figure 5-3.

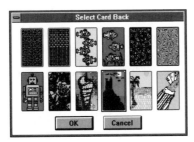

FIGURE 5-3. *Solitaire's available card backs.*

2. Select the desired card back and then choose OK.

Starting a New Game

To start a new game, choose Deal from the Game menu. Solitaire shuffles the cards and deals.

Optional Rules

In addition to straight Solitaire, you can select Standard or Vegas scoring rules. To select the scoring rules, choose Options from the Game menu. A dialog box similar to the one shown in Figure 5-4 appears.

The Draw radio buttons control how Solitaire deals cards from the available card pile: either one card at a time, or three cards at a time. The Timed game check box lets you turn Solitaire's game timer on or off. The Status bar check box lets you turn on or off the status bar Solitaire uses to display the score and timer. The Outline dragging check box controls whether the entire card or only the card's outline is displayed when you drag it.

FIGURE 5-4. *The Options dialog box.*

In Standard scoring, Solitaire scores the game as follows:

- +5 points for any card moved from the deck to a card column.
- +10 points for any card played onto a suit stack.
- −15 points for moving a card from a suit stack to a card column.
- −20 points for each pass, after three passes, with the Draw Three option.
- −100 points for each pass, after one pass, with the Draw One option.

In Vegas scoring, Solitaire scores the game as follows:

- Your initial wager is $52.00.
- You win $5.00 for each card you place in a suit stack.
- You get only one pass through the card deck with the Draw One option.
- You get only three passes through the card deck with the Draw Three option.

PLAYING MINESWEEPER

Minesweeper is a board game that combines chance and skill. To play Minesweeper, expand the Minesweeper icon in the Games group window. A window similar to Figure 5-5 appears.

FIGURE 5-5. *The Minesweeper game board.*

The board, initially an 8×8 grid, contains 10 mines. Your goal is to identify the location of each mine.

To begin, click on a square. If the square contains a mine, the location of each mine is revealed and the game is over, as shown in Figure 5-6.

FIGURE 5-6. *An unsuccessful game.*

If the square isn't a mine, a number appears, as shown in Figure 5-7.

FIGURE 5-7. *An uncovered square.*

Each square is surrounded by up to eight other squares. The number Minesweeper displays in an uncovered square is the number of mines in the squares surrounding the uncovered square. For example, there are two mines in the eight squares that surround the uncovered square in Figure 5-7. By combining your knowledge about the number of mines in the surrounding squares, you can narrow down the squares that you think contain mines. Do not click on a square that you think contains a mine. Doing so would explode the mine and end the game. Instead, click on the square using the right mouse button. This marks the square with a flag, as shown in Figure 5-8.

If you are not sure whether a location contains a mine, you can double-click on the square using the right mouse button. A question mark appears in the square. After you make other moves, you can change the question mark into a flag if you think the square contains a mine, or you can click on the square with the left mouse button to uncover it.

FIGURE 5-8. *Marking a suspected mine location.*

Minesweeper has four levels:

Beginner	64 squares, 10 mines
Intermediate	256 squares, 40 mines
Expert	480 squares, 99 mines
Custom	User defined

Choose the level you want from the Game menu.

Minesweeper keeps track of the fastest time at each level. If you have the fastest time for your level, Minesweeper displays a dialog box asking you to type in your name.

APPENDIX A

Installing Windows

This section helps you if you need to install Windows. Note that before you can continue, you must be using MS-DOS version 3.1 or later. The instructions throughout this book assume you are using MS-DOS 5 or later.

HARDWARE REQUIREMENTS FOR WINDOWS 3.1

To use Windows 3.1, you need

- An IBM-PC–compatible computer with an 80286, 80386, 80386SX, i486, i486SX, or compatible microprocessor
- 1 MB or more of memory (640 KB of conventional memory plus 384 KB of extended memory)
- A hard disk with 8 to 10 MB (or more) of available storage
- An EGA, VGA, 8514/A, or compatible graphics adapter and monitor (VGA or higher recommended)
- A mouse (not necessary, but highly recommended)

INSTALLING WINDOWS

To begin the Windows installation, place Windows installation floppy disk 1 in drive A, and use the following command to change to drive A:

```
C:\>A: <Enter>
```

Then use the following command to run Setup:

```
A:\>SETUP <Enter>
```

Information then appears about the Windows installation. Read the information, and press Enter to continue. Setup displays a screen asking if you want to perform an Express Setup or a Custom Setup. Unless you're an experienced computer user, press Enter to choose an Express Setup.

Setup then checks your computer's configuration. If Setup detects network software, Setup might inform you that a newer version of your network software is available.

Setup prompts you for the directory to which you want to install Windows 3.1. If you're upgrading from Windows 3.0 or installing Windows for the first time, simply press Enter.

Next, Setup begins copying files onto your hard disk, occasionally asking you to insert the other installation disks. Insert each disk as directed and press Enter.

Eventually a dialog box appears, similar to the one shown in Figure A-1. Type your name and your company's name (if applicable) into the text boxes, and then choose OK. Setup asks you to confirm your choices, and then continues installing Windows.

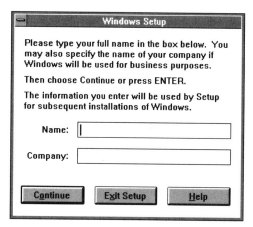

FIGURE A-1. *Setup asks you to type in your name and your company's name.*

Selecting a Printer

As the installation continues, Setup asks you to select a printer. Printer selection is actually a two-step process: First you select the printer attached to your computer, and then you configure it. This section describes this process.

A dialog box appears, similar to the one shown in Figure A-2, requesting that you select a printer.

1. Use the arrow keys to scroll through the printer list and highlight your printer. (To speed up this process, type the first letter of your

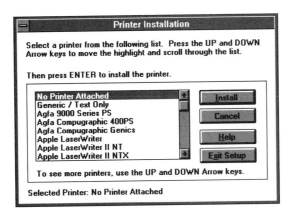

FIGURE A-2. *The Printer Installation dialog box.*

printer's name.) If your printer's name does not appear, highlight
Install Unlisted or Updated Printer.

2. Choose OK.

3. Setup might ask you to insert another disk. Do so and press Enter.

After you've selected a printer, a dialog box appears, asking you to
select the port to which the printer is attached, as shown in Figure A-3.
Select a port from the list box and choose Install.

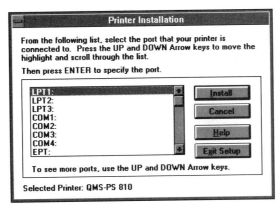

FIGURE A-3. *The Printer Installation dialog box.*

Setting Up Applications

After you select and configure your printer, Setup begins searching
your hard disk for applications. A dialog box appears, similar to the one
shown in Figure A-4.

FIGURE A-4. *The Windows Setup dialog box.*

If Setup finds an application it can't identify, it asks you to select the application, as shown in Figure A-5.

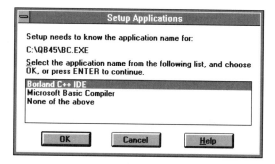

FIGURE A-5. *Setup asks you to select an application it can't identify.*

Select the application's name and choose OK.

After searching for applications, Setup displays a dialog box similar to the one shown in Figure A-6 asking if you want to run the Windows tutorial. The tutorial introduces you to mouse and window operations.

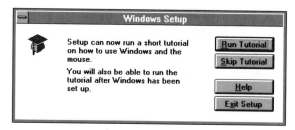

FIGURE A-6. *Setup asks if you want to run the tutorial.*

If you are new to Windows, choose Run Tutorial to run the tutorial. If you don't want to run the tutorial, choose Skip Tutorial. Setup continues the installation. Part I of this reference shows you how to run the tutorial at a later time from within Windows.

Completing the Windows Installation

The Windows installation is now complete. Setup displays a dialog box similar to the one shown in Figure A-7.

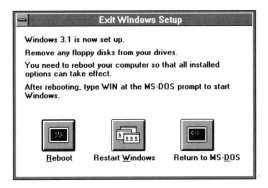

FIGURE A-7. *The Exit Windows Setup dialog box.*

If you want to start Windows, choose the Restart Windows button. If you want to return to the MS-DOS prompt, choose the Return to MS-DOS button. (Choose the Reboot button if you don't see a Restart Windows button.)

WHICH MODE IS RIGHT FOR YOU?

Windows runs in one of two modes: Standard or 386 Enhanced mode. The mode is dictated by your computer type and the amount of memory your computer contains. The following table describes the minimum CPU and memory requirements for each operating mode:

Mode	CPU	Memory
Standard	80286	1 MB (640 KB conventional, plus 384 KB extended)
386 Enhanced	80386SX, 80386, i486SX, i486	2 MB (640 KB conventional, plus 1024 KB extended)

Each mode provides Windows with a certain degree of power. The following paragraphs provide a brief description of each mode and its capabilities.

Standard Mode

Windows automatically runs in standard mode on computers that use the Intel 80286 microprocessor (or an equivalent microprocessor) and have 640 KB of conventional memory and at least 384 KB of extended memory. Standard mode lets you start and run as many Windows-based applications as you'd like, limited by the amount of your computer's available memory. You can run applications designed for MS-DOS as well, but applications designed for MS-DOS must use the full screen and run in the foreground only.

386 Enhanced Mode

386 Enhanced mode is the most powerful operating mode available with Windows. Windows automatically runs in 386 Enhanced mode on computers with an 80386SX, 80386, i486SX, or i486 microprocessor (or equivalent microprocessors) with 640 KB of conventional memory and at least 1024 KB of extended memory.

In 386 Enhanced mode, Windows can treat free space on your hard drive as extra memory. (This is known as *virtual memory.*) In 386 Enhanced mode, you can start and run as many Windows-based applications as you'd like, limited by the amount of your computer's available memory. 386 Enhanced mode also lets applications designed for MS-DOS run in the full screen or in a window.

APPENDIX B
Fundamental Keys in Windows

In Windows 3.1 you can perform a number of tasks with a few simple key combinations. Figure B-1 lists the key combinations you typically use within a window. Figure B-2 lists key combinations you commonly use within a dialog box.

Key(s)	Function
Alt+Spacebar	Opens an application window's Control menu
Alt+Hyphen	Opens a document window's Control menu
Alt+F4	Closes the active application window
Alt+Esc	Selects the next application window or icon
Alt+Tab	Allows you to perform fast switching between applications
Alt+Print Screen	Copies an image of the active window onto the Clipboard
Ctrl+Esc	Opens the Task List
Ctrl+Tab	Activates the next group or document window
Ctrl+F4	Closes the active group or document window
Shift+F1	Activates context-sensitive help on a specific command or screen element. This is only available with some applications designed for Windows
F1	Activates online help
Print Screen	Copies the current screen image to the Clipboard

FIGURE B-1. *Fundamental key combinations used in Windows.*

Key(s)	Function
Alt+*X*	Selects the element noted by *X* (the letter underlined on screen)
Alt+Down arrow	Opens the selected drop-down list
Alt+Up arrow	Selects an item in a drop-down list
Alt+F4 or Esc	Cancels a dialog box
Ctrl+/	Selects all items in the contents pane of a File Manager window
Ctrl+\	Cancels all items in the contents pane of a File Manager window
Shift+Tab	Moves to the previous field
Tab	Moves to the next field
Home	Moves to the first character in a text box
End	Moves to the last character in a text box
Enter	Executes a command
Spacebar	Selects or cancels a check box item
F10	Selects the first menu on the menu bar

FIGURE B-2. *Fundamental key combinations used in dialog boxes.*

APPENDIX C

Memory and System Settings

This section provides information concerning memory types and uses as well as information concerning system settings that you can change with the Setup application.

PUTTING MEMORY TO WORK

NOTE: *Memory is too complex a subject to cover fully here. For a lively and useful guide to taking full advantage of your computer's memory, see Dan Gookin's* The Microsoft Guide to Managing Memory with DOS 5 *(Microsoft Press, 1991).*

Your computer can contain as many as three types of memory: *conventional memory, extended memory,* and *expanded memory.* All IBM-PC–compatible computers have conventional memory, which is memory up to 640 KB (although some computers have less than the 640-KB amount).

If your computer uses an 80286, 80386, 80386SX, i486SX, or i486 microprocessor, it probably contains extended memory. Extended memory is memory above the 1-MB mark. Computers that use the 8088 or 8086 microprocessors cannot have extended memory. As a general rule, the more extended memory you add to your computer, the faster Windows runs your applications.

Expanded memory is essentially a pool of extra memory. Using a special memory board and software, expanded memory can be mapped into a 64-KB region of *upper memory* (within the 384-KB memory area between 640 KB and 1 MB). Different areas of expanded memory can be mapped into this 64-KB region. All IBM-PC–compatible computers can use expanded memory.

If you are using an 80286-based, 80386SX-based, 80386-based, i486SX-based, or i486-based computer that has extended memory, be sure that your CONFIG.SYS file loads HIMEM.SYS, which is an extended memory manager (provided with Windows and MS-DOS 5) that lets your computer use extended memory. Check to ensure that a line similar to the following appears in your CONFIG.SYS file:

```
DEVICE=C:\DOS\HIMEM.SYS
```

If you are using an 80386SX-based, 80386-based, i486SX-based, or i486-based computer and you use an application that needs expanded memory, be sure that your CONFIG.SYS file loads EMM386.EXE. EMM386.EXE uses extended memory to simulate expanded memory. Check to ensure that a line similar to the following appears in your CONFIG.SYS file:

```
DEVICE=C:\DOS\EMM386.EXE
```

Creating a RAM Disk

Many Windows-based applications create temporary files. You can improve the performance of Windows by creating a RAM disk and storing temporary files there.

To create a RAM disk, add the following line to your CONFIG.SYS file:

```
DEVICE=C:\DOS\RAMDRIVE.SYS  [DiskSize [SectorSize [DirectoryEntries]]]
[/A ¦ /E]
```

Items shown in square brackets are optional. Items separated by the pipe (¦) character are mutually exclusive—that is, you can use only one or the other.

- *DiskSize* specifies the RAM disk's size in kilobytes, from 16 (16 KB) through 4096 (4096 KB). The default value is 64 (64 KB).

- *SectorSize* specifies the size of the RAM disk's sectors. A large sector size is good for large files, and a small sector size is good for small files. Valid numbers for *SectorSize* are 128, 256, 512, or 1024. The default value is 512 (512 KB). If you specify *SectorSize*, you must also specify *DiskSize*.

- *DirectoryEntries* specifies the maximum number of files the RAM disk's root directory can hold, from 2 through 1024. The default is 64 (64 entries). If you provide a value for *DirectoryEntries*, you must also specify *SectorSize* and *DiskSize*.

- The /A and /E switches control the type of memory used to create the RAM disk. Specify /A to use expanded memory or /E to use extended memory. If you do not specify /A or /E, the RAM disk is created in conventional memory.

Creating a Disk Cache

A *disk cache* is a large buffer in memory that holds information that has been written on disk. If an application needs to read that information, it reads it from the disk cache instead of from the disk, thereby improving the computer's performance.

To create a disk cache, add the following line to your AUTOEXEC.BAT file and then reboot your computer:

```
C:\WINDOWS\SMARTDRV.EXE
```

This line sets up a basic disk cache. If you're familiar with MS-DOS commands, SMARTDRV.EXE has a number of optional parameters for fine-tuning its performance. The complete syntax for SMARTDRV.EXE is as follows:

```
C:\WINDOWS\SMARTDRV.EXE [[/E:ElementSize] [/B:BufferSize]
  [DriveLetter [+] ¦ [-]] [Size] [WinSize]]...
```

Parameters shown in square brackets are optional. Parameters separated by the pipe character (¦) are mutually exclusive—that is, you can use only one of them. The ellipsis (...) indicates that the parameters can be repeated, allowing you to specify disk caching for more than one disk drive.

- */E:ElementSize* is the size of the disk cache elements (in bytes)
- */B:BufferSize* is the size of the read buffer
- *DriveLetter* is the letter of the disk drive you are caching
- + enables write-behind caching for the specified disk drive
- − disables all caching for the specified disk drive
- *Size* is the amount of extended memory (in kilobytes) used by the disk cache. The default value depends on the amount of memory in your computer
- *WinSize* is the amount of extended memory (in kilobytes) used by the disk cache when Windows is running. The default value depends on the amount of memory in your computer
- */C* writes all write-behind information onto the hard disk
- */R* clears the contents of the existing disk cache and restarts SMARTDRV.EXE
- */L* loads SMARTDRV.EXE into low memory

- ■ /Q prevents the display of SMARTDRV.EXE information on your screen

- ■ /S displays additional information about the status of SMARTDRV.EXE

CHANGING SYSTEM SETTINGS USING SETUP

If you change your video card, mouse, keyboard, or network, you must tell Windows about the change. To do this, expand the Program Manager's Setup icon. A dialog box similar to the one shown in Figure C-1 appears that lists your existing system settings.

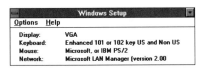

FIGURE C-1. *The Windows Setup dialog box.*

The Setup application lets you perform two different tasks: changing system settings and setting up applications.

Changing System Settings

To change your system settings, choose Change System Settings from the Options menu. A dialog box similar to the one shown in Figure C-2 appears.

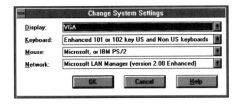

FIGURE C-2. *The Change System Settings dialog box.*

This dialog box has drop-down list boxes for Display, Keyboard, Mouse, and Network. To change a setting, follow these steps:

1. Select the setting, and open its drop-down list box.

2. Choose the new setting.

3. Windows might ask you to insert one or more Windows disks. Follow the instructions on the screen.

4. After you finish changing settings, choose OK. A dialog box appears that prompts you to restart Windows or return to MS-DOS. To do so, choose the appropriate icon.

Adding Applications Designed for MS-DOS

If you have one or more applications designed for MS-DOS, you can let Setup search your hard disk for these applications and create an icon for each. To do this, choose Set Up Applications from the Options menu. A dialog box similar to the one shown in Figure C-3 appears.

FIGURE C-3. *The Setup Applications dialog box.*

Choose OK to let Setup search for all applications designed for MS-DOS. The dialog box changes to resemble Figure C-4.

FIGURE C-4. *The Setup Applications dialog box.*

By default, Setup searches all directories listed in the Path command in your AUTOEXEC.BAT file. To search a specific drive, select the desired drive in the list box. Choose Search Now to begin the search. As Setup searches, a dialog box similar to the one shown in Figure C-5 appears.

FIGURE C-5. *The Windows Setup dialog box.*

Setup occasionally finds an application designed for MS-DOS that it can't identify. If so, Setup displays a dialog box similar to Figure C-6.

Select the correct application in the list box and choose OK. Setup continues its search.

After Setup has completed the search, a dialog box similar to the one shown in Figure C-7 appears.

FIGURE C-6. *An unidentified application designed for MS-DOS.*

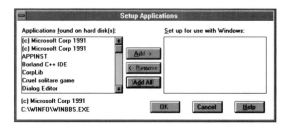

FIGURE C-7. *The expanded Setup Applications dialog box.*

The dialog box displays all the applications found in the search. To add all the applications, choose Add All. To add specific applications, follow these steps:

1. Select the application from the Applications Found On Hard Disk(s) list box.

2. Choose Add.

If you change your mind about adding an application, follow these steps:

1. Select the application from the Set Up For Use With Windows list box.

2. Choose Remove.

3. After you finish selecting applications, choose OK.

Setup really doesn't prepare an application designed for MS-DOS for running under Windows. Instead, it adds an icon for the application to the Applications group. For more information on running applications designed for MS-DOS, refer to the description of the PIF Editor in Part II.

Removing Optional Windows Components

Windows places several documentation files and Windows accessory programs on your hard disk as well as a variety of wallpaper files. You don't need these files to run Windows. If your hard disk is running out of room, you might want to remove one of these optional components.

To remove one of these components, follow these steps:

1. Expand the Windows Setup icon in the Main group window.

2. Choose Add/Remove Windows Components from the Options menu. A dialog box similar to the one shown in Figure C-8 appears.

3. Deselect the component to remove it. If you want to remove specific files within a component, choose Files for that component. A dialog box similar to the one shown in Figure C-9 appears.

4. Select the files you want to remove in the Install These Files On Hard Disk list box, and then choose Remove. Choose OK.

5. Choose OK in the Windows Setup dialog box. Windows asks you to confirm any deletions.

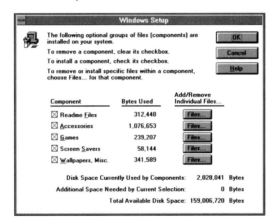

FIGURE C-8. *The Windows Setup dialog box.*

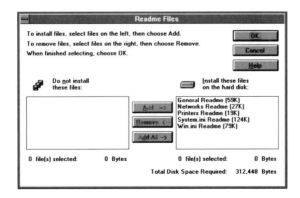

FIGURE C-9. *A dialog box from which you can add and remove files.*

APPENDIX D

Glossary

Below are definitions of common terms used throughout this book. For a complete computer dictionary, see the *Microsoft Press Computer Dictionary* (Microsoft Press, 1991).

Active window The window you are currently working in, or have just selected. The active window is the topmost window.

Application A computer program that performs a specific task, such as word processing.

Application window The primary window for an application. An application window might contain multiple document windows.

Associate To identify a filename extension as belonging to a certain application. The File Manager lets you define associations.

Check box A small square box that appears within a dialog box, which when selected contains an X, and when deselected is empty.

Command button A large button within a dialog box that either cancels or carries out the selected command.

Control menu The menu represented by a horizontal bar in the upper left-hand corner of every window. The Control menu lets you size, move, or close the window.

Default printer The printer Windows automatically uses when you choose Print. Windows allows only one default printer.

Desktop The screen background upon which Windows displays windows, icons, and dialog boxes.

Dialog box A rectangular box from which Windows either displays or requests information.

Document Any information you create with an application and save.

Document window A window within an application window. Each document window contains a single document.

Drop-down list box A single-line list box entry that opens to reveal a list of choices.

Font A graphic design applied to a collection of numerals, symbols, and characters in the alphabet.

Font set A collection of font sizes for a specified font.

Font style An emphasis applied to a font, such as bold or italic.

Group A collection of applications within the Program Manager. The Program Manager lets you create, access, and manage groups.

Group window A Program Manager window that displays items within a group.

Icon A graphical representation of an object.

List box A type of information box within a dialog box that contains a list of choices.

MCI (Media Control Interface) The software that provides a device-independent multimedia interface.

Menu A list of available commands in an application window.

Menu bar The horizontal bar at the top of an application window, immediately beneath the title bar, which lists the available menus.

MIDI (Musical Instrument Digital Interface) An interface that allows communication between several computers, devices, or musical instruments.

Minimize button A small button to the right of a Windows title bar containing a downward-pointing arrow. The Minimize button minimizes the window to an icon.

Multimedia The combined use of text, graphics, video, and sound to present information to a user.

Non-Windows application An application that was not written to run in Windows.

Object Any piece of information created using a Windows-based application.

Option button A small round button within a dialog box used to select an option. Within a group of related option buttons, you can select only one button.

Package An icon that represents either embedded or linked information.

Restore button A small button to the right of a Windows title bar that contains an up arrow and a down arrow. The Restore button returns a maximized window to its previous size.

Scroll bar A bar along the right edge or bottom of a window that lets you scroll the contents of a window or list box to display information not currently visible.

Shortcut key A key or key combination that when pressed executes a specific command without the user first selecting the command from a menu.

Status bar A horizontal bar beneath a window that displays status information.

Task List A window containing a list of all the currently running applications from which you can quickly switch to another application.

Text box A dialog box entry within which you can type text, such as a filename.

Title bar The horizontal bar at the top of a window or dialog box containing the title of the window or dialog box.

Track A sound sequence on a compact disk that typically corresponds to a song.

TrueType fonts Fonts that are scalable and print exactly as they appear on your screen.

WAV The filename extension associated with files containing Wave (waveform) data.

Window A rectangular, framed area on your screen, within which you can display an application or document.

Windows application An application written to run in Windows.

Index

Kris Jamsa

Kris Jamsa is the author of over 40 computer books written on a wide range of topics including MS-DOS, hard-disk management, MS-DOS batch files, Microsoft Windows, graphics, programming languages, WordPerfect, and WordPerfect for Windows. Many of Jamsa's books have appeared on bestseller lists across the country and collectively have sold over one million copies.

Jamsa grew up in Seattle and moved to Phoenix, Arizona, for high school. He received his bachelor's degree in computer science from the United States Air Force Academy in 1983. After graduation, Jamsa worked in Las Vegas as a VAX/VMS system manager for the Air Force. In 1986 he received his master's degree in computer science from the University of Nevada at Las Vegas. Jamsa left the Air Force in 1988 to write full time. He is currently a Ph.D. candidate at Arizona State University, researching multiprocessor operating systems.

He currently lives in Las Vegas with his wife, Debbie, their daughters, Stephanie and Kellie, and Happy, their dalmatian puppy.

The manuscript for this book was prepared and submitted to Microsoft Press in electronic form. Text files were processed and formatted using Microsoft Word.

Principal editorial compositor: Barb Runyan
Principal typographer: Ruth Pettis
Interior text designer: Kim Eggleston
Principal illustrators: Peggy Herman and Lisa Sandburg
Cover designer: Rikki Conrad Design
Cover color separator: Color Service

Text composition by Microsoft Press in Times Roman with display type in Futura Heavy, using the Magna composition system and the Linotronic 300 laser imagesetter.

Great Resources for Windows™ 3.1 Users

LEARNING & RUNNING WINDOWS™ 3.1
Includes *Microsoft® Productivity Pack for Windows 3.1* and *Running Windows 3.1, 3rd ed.*
Microsoft Corporation and Craig Stinson

This is the ideal blending of software and book instruction for users of all levels of experience.
If you want to be up and running with Windows 3.1 quickly and easily, this is the place to start.
The *Microsoft Productivity Pack for Windows 3.1* (regularly $59.95) combines disk-based lessons
with hands-on exercises. Guided practice sessions and concise explanations help you master the
basics of Windows. RUNNING WINDOWS 3.1 (regularly $27.95) will continue to answer your
day-to-day questions about Windows long after you've learned the basics from the software
tutorial. An unbeatable package at an unbeatable price. Sold separately for $87.90.
608 pages, softcover with one 5¹/₂-inch (HD) disk $39.95 ($54.95 Canada)

RUNNING WINDOWS™ 3.1, 3rd ed.
Craig Stinson

Build your confidence and enhance your productivity with Microsoft Windows, quickly and
easily, using this hands-on introduction. This Microsoft-authorized edition—for new as well as
experienced Windows users—is completely updated and expanded to cover all the new exciting
features of version 3.1. You'll find a successful combination of step-by-step tutorials, helpful
screen illustrations, expert tips, and real-world examples. Learn how to install and start using
Windows 3.1, use applications with Windows, and maximize Windows performance.
608 pages, softcover $27.95 ($37.95 Canada)

WINDOWS™ 3.1 COMPANION
The Cobb Group: Lori L. Lorenz and R. Michael O'Mara with Russell Borland

*"Covers the basics thoroughly... An excellent reference featuring dozens of live examples...
Beautifully produced."* **PC Magazine**
This up-to-date resource thoroughly covers Windows version 3.1—everything from installing
and starting Windows to using all its built-in applications and desktop accessories. Step-by-step
tutorials, great examples, and expert advice for novices to advanced users.
550 pages, softcover $27.95 ($37.95 Canada)

*Microsoft Press books are available wherever quality computer books are sold.
Or call **1-800-MSPRESS** for ordering information or placing credit card orders.*
Please refer to **BBK** when placing your order. Prices subject to change.*

* In Canada, contact Macmillan Canada, Attn: Microsoft Press Dept., 164 Commander Blvd., Agincourt, Ontario, Canada M1S 3C7,
or call (416) 293-8141.
In the U.K., contact Microsoft Press, 27 Wrights Lane, London W8 5TZ.

Outstanding Word for Windows Resources

MICROSOFT® WORD FOR WINDOWS™ STEP BY STEP
Version 2
Microsoft Corporation

MICROSOFT WORD FOR WINDOWS STEP BY STEP shows you how Word can
make your everyday work easy. Whether you're new to word processing or new to Microsoft
Word for Windows, you'll learn to produce professional-quality documents with ease. This
timesaving package—now updated for version 2—includes disk-basked tutorials with follow-along
lessons and practice exercises. Each lesson includes clear objectives, step-by-step instructions,
useful tips, disk-based practice files, plus handy tips, and advice. And the lessons are progressive
yet modular, so the novice user can advance from one lesson to the next, and the intermediate user
can jump in at any point. This is the perfect training guide for business, classroom, or home use.
292 pages, softcover with one 5¹/₄-inch disk $29.95 ($39.95 Canada)

WORD FOR WINDOWS™ COMPANION, 2nd ed.
The Cobb Group: Mark W. Crane with M. David Stone and Alfred Poor

WORD FOR WINDOWS COMPANION makes Word for Windows easy to learn and use.
Regardless of your level of expertise, you'll find a wealth of useful information in this comprehensive
resource—now updated for version 2. It's both an exceptional tutorial for new Word for Windows
users and a master reference guide for experienced users. You'll learn basic concepts of word processing,
typography, and design that you can use to create professional-looking documents with confidence and ease.
In addition to detailed explanations, the book offers scores of illustrations, examples, and tips to enhance
your productivity. An extensive index and side-margin headings make information readily accessible.
896 pages, softcover $27.95 ($37.95 Canada)   Available May 1992

RUNNING WORD FOR WINDOWS™
Version 2
Russell Borland

This example-rich book is an outstanding reference for intermediate and advanced Microsoft
Word for Windows users. Now completely updated, it highlights all the powerful new features
of Word for Windows version 2. This book moves from a review of the basics to a full description
of Word's power-packed features: styles, fields, macros, and templates. Throughout, special tips
provide additional insight and suggest handy shortcuts. You'll discover the most effective—and
easiest—ways to produce professional-looking documents. You won't find a more authoritative
or comprehensive source of information than RUNNING WORD FOR WINDOWS.
592 pages, softcover $27.95 ($34.95 Canada)